GW00401808

pasta

contents

introduction

Pasta in all its forms has graced tables across Italy, and indeed all over the globe, for thousands of years. Recognised as one of the world's most beloved foods, pasta possesses qualities that quite possibly will make it the twenty-first century's food of choice.

Pasta's superior nutritional benefits have earned it 'superfood' status. It's also the ideal staple: economical, easy to store and prepare, versatile and highly pleasurable to eat. In fact, one could easily call pasta 'the perfect food'.

PASTA FRESH AND DRIED

Pasta is made from grain combined with liquid (and sometimes other ingredients for flavouring and colouring). Kneading produces a smooth dough or paste (hence the word pasta), that can be rolled out or cut and formed into any of hundreds of varieties. Making sense of the multitude of pasta varieties is simplified by dividing pasta into two categories: fresh and dried (see page 9).

BASIC INGREDIENTS

The basic ingredients of fresh pasta are flour and eggs, with perhaps a little oil or water added to make the dough easier to work with, plus some salt for flavour.

Most commercially produced dried pasta is made from water and semolina – a special kind of flour ground from high quality durum wheat. Semolina creates a firm, elastic dough that's sturdy enough to be shaped by a machine.

Semolina can also be used in homemade pasta, either alone or mixed with plain flour, to strengthen the dough and enhance the texture of the final product.

NUTRITIONAL VALUE

Pasta is valued as a high-energy, low-fat food and a high source of dietary fibre. It supplies moderate amounts of protein and some B Group vitamins, especially thiamine.

The sauces served with pasta increase the nutritive content. With an informed choice, fat content can remain low, making pasta meals ideal for healthy eating.

Different thicknesses of dried pasta require different cooking times. It should also be noted that fresh pasta, with its higher moisture content, usually cooks much more quickly than even the thinnest dried pasta.

TIPS

When cooked, immediately drain the pasta. Don't rinse it, unless the directions specifically say so, as washing reduces the nutrients in the meal.

Always sauce the pasta at once to keep it from sticking, tossing well to distribute the sauce evenly. Pasta that is to be sauced and baked should be undercooked slightly, otherwise it will be too soft after baking.

With spaghetti, apply a light sauce to a fine stick, such as angel-hair, and a more robust sauce to a thicker strand. A rule of thumb is to ensure the sauce grades increase with the thickness of the spaghetti, linguine or fettuccine used. When using tubular pasta, try a clinging sauce that will stick both inside and out. Shell-shaped pasta is just right for holding puddles of sauce and pieces of meat, fish or poultry.

Twists are more versatile as they allow a robust sauce to wrap around them for a full–flavoured dish, and can accept a light vinaigrette when served in a cold salad.

Sauce ingredients are only limited by your imagination and desire to experiment. We've included a number of very tasty sauces throughout this book, however, we encourage you to experiment and experience the delight of creating your own marvellous dish using your favourite pasta as a base.

THE BEST OILS FOR PASTA

The subtle flavour of pasta is enhanced by good quality olive oil. The flavour and quality of olive oil varies according to the type of olives it was pressed from, where the olives were grown and the method of pressing. Olive oils are graded according to how much oleic acid they contain and the procedure used to make them. The oil must be pressed from olives that were not chemically treated in order to qualify for one of the following top four categories:

- Virgin (no more than 4% oleic acid)
- Fine virgin (no more than 3% oleic acid)
- Caster virgin (no more than 2% oleic acid)
- Extra virgin (no more than 1% oleic acid)

STORING AND USING OLIVE OIL

- Choose olive oil with a clean, fruity aroma, full body and fruity or peppery flavour.
- Store olive oil away from heat and light, which can cause it to become rancid (use within a year's time).
- Use a good-tasting, affordable olive oil for sautéed and baked dishes. Save the finest grades for pesto and other uncooked dishes or for drizzling over cooked foods just before serving.

Types of Pasta

Pasta is the generic Italian name for many noodle-like pastes or doughs that are made into a wide variety of shapes and sizes. There are far too many different kinds than can be counted. The two main types are fresh pasta (pasta fresca) and dried pasta (pasta secca).

Fresh egg pasta is the most common fresh pasta and can be homemade or store-bought. Dried pasta is far less expensive to produce and keeps well in a hot, dry climate. In southern Italy, fresh stuffed pasta such as ravioli and cannelloni are served more for holidays and special occasions. Italians don't compare fresh egg pasta to dried pasta: one is not considered better than the other. They are simply different and the sauces that accompany them should respect that difference.

FRESH PASTA

The fresh pasta that enjoys uncontested recognition as Italy's finest is that of Emilia-Romagna. Here melted butter accented with sage is a common sauce. Cream sauces are popular also and vegetable and light tomato sauces are made during the warmer months. The basic dough for homemade fresh pasta consists of eggs and plain flour. No salt, olive oil or water is added. The only other ingredient that may be used is spinach or Swiss chard for green pasta dough.

Fresh egg pasta is often cut into strands that vary in width, such as fettuccine, pappardelle and lasagne. It is also filled with meat, cheese or vegetables to create ravioli, tortellini and cannelloni. In Emilia-Romagna, where Parmigiano-Reggiano is also made, freshly grated cheese is usually grated over the completed dish.

Fresh pasta can also be made without eggs. In Apulia, semolina flour is mixed with water and shaped into orecchiette, which is pinched with the thumb, or cavatelli, which is rolled into a cylinder. In Sicily, it is also rolled around a knitting needle to make fusilli. The Sicilians also make a fresh pasta for cavatelli or gnocchi that is made from flour mixed with ricotta cheese.

Fresh pasta can be dried and stored at room temperature, but it is important that the pasta is completely dried before storing. Fresh pasta is more delicate than dried pasta, making it more difficult to store.

DRIED PASTA

Dried pasta is also sometimes referred to as factory-made pasta. The finest dried pasta is made from golden semolina flour ground from durum wheat and mixed with water. Once shaped, the pasta must be fully dried before it can be packaged. Good quality dried pasta should have a slightly rough surface and compact body that maintains its firmness in cooking, since it swells considerably in size when cooked.

Typical sauces for dried pasta are based on olive oil rather than butter. But as some of the recipes bear out, there are several butter-based sauces that combine well with dried pasta. In southern Italy, dried pasta is most often married with a tomato sauce, which may be plain or with meat, seafood or vegetables.

TAGLIATELLE [FRESH AND DRY]

Another of the flat ribbon pastas, tagliatelle is eaten more in northern Italy than in the south and is used in the same ways as fettuccine. It is a long thin, ribbon pasta that is generally found ¼in (7.5mm) in width. It can be made with or without eggs.

SPAGHETTI [FRESH AND DRY]

Deriving its name from the Italian word 'spago', meaning 'string', spaghetti is the most popular and best known pasta outside of Italy. It can be simply served with butter or oil and is good with almost any sauce.

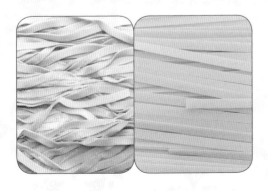

FETTUCCINE [FRESH AND DRY]

A flat ribbon pasta that's used in a similar way to spaghetti. Often sold coiled in nests, fettuccine is particularly good with creamy sauces, which cling better than heavier sauces.

PAPPARDELLE

This very wide ribbon pasta was traditionally served with a sauce of hare, herbs and wine, but today it is teamed with any rich sauce.

LINGUINE

This long, thin pasta looks somewhat like spaghetti but has square-cut ends. It can be used in the same way as spaghetti, fettuccine and tagliatelle.

MAFALDINE

Also called margherita and similar to tripolini pasta. A flat ribbon pasta that is a slightly narrower version of the long variety of mafalda. It is approximately ¼in (1cm) in width and like mafalda it can have a rippled edge on one or both sides. It is also sometimes referred to as riccia.

ANGEL-HAIR PASTA
Also called 'capelli di angelo', this is an extremely long thin pasta that's dried in coils to prevent it from breaking. Because of its delicate nature, angel-hair pasta is best served with a light sauce.

ZITI
These come either as long, hollow rods or as short tubes, called cut ziti. It's often baked in a casserole.
Substitutions: Rigatoni, penne, elbow macaroni, mostaccioli, ditali, ditalini and elicoidali.

CANNELLONI
This large, hollow pasta is most often stuffed, topped with sauce and cheese, then baked. Cannelloni can also be stuffed and deep-fried until crisp. If deep-frying, the tubes need to be boiled before stuffing and frying.

LASAGNE

These flat sheets of pasta are most often layered with a meat, fish or vegetable sauce, topped with cheese, then baked to make a delicious and satisfying dish. Instant lasagne that you don't have to cook before using is also available.

RAVIOLI

Composed of a filling sealed between two layers of pasta dough. Ravioli are commonly rectangular or circular in shape and stuffed with meat, ricotta cheese or vegetables such as spinach and nettles. The filling could also be potatoes, squash or even tofu. Though often topped with a tomato-based sauce, the sauces are as varied as the fillings. Pesto, broth and cream-based sauces are also common.

CAPPELLETTI

Egg-filled pasta made by using a 2¼in (6cm) square of pasta. If bigger and irregular it is known as cappellacci, which is usually stuffed with pumpkin and ricotta cheese.

AGNOLOTTI

A pasta filled with various ingredients that is made as a circle or square of pasta dough folded over and sealed on the open edge to form a half circle or rectangular shape. Similar to ravioli, agnolotti pasta is stuffed with various ingredients, such as meats and cheeses. Substitutions: Cappelletti, ravioli and tortellini.

TORTELLINI

A ring-shaped pasta typically stuffed with a mix of meat (pork loin, prosciutto, mortadella) and Parmesan cheese. Originally from the Italian region of Emilia (in particular Bologna and Modena), they are usually served in broth, with cream or with a ragù or similar sauce.

CAVATELLI

A small shell-shaped pasta that has slightly rolled-in edges. The name is sometimes associated with pasta that is similar in shape to casarecce, only shorter in length, but most often it refers to the small shell-shaped pasta. It is good to serve with thick, chunky, meat sauces. Substitutions: Casarecce, cicatelli, gnocchetti or rotini.

CORTECCE

A stringy style pasta with a rough surface which can easily absorb a cooking sauce.

GNOCCHI

In the Italian tradition gnocchi are always meant to be dumplings. They are generally made from a potato base with the addition of flour. The proportions of potatoes and flour may vary from one region to another.

GNOCCHI TRICOLOUR

In addition to potato-based gnocchi, there are also other types of gnocchi made with flour, semolina, ricotta cheese, spinach or breadcrumbs. Gnocchetti are usually smaller than gnocchi.

PENNE

A short, tubular pasta, similar to macaroni, but with ends cut at an angle rather than straight. It's particularly suited to being served with meat and heavier sauces that catch in the hollows.

Substitutes: Mostaccioli (shorter, wider tubes), ziti (break into small pieces if in long form), rigatoni, elbow macaroni (use one-third less if measuring by volume), elicoidali, ditali and fusilli.

TORTIGLIONI

Similar to penne, though the diameter is a little greater (¼in/1cm) and the ridging is less dense and spirals around rather than going straight up their sides. Also, it's cut straight rather than at a slant. It is good to serve with thick, chunky sauces and baked pasta dishes.

Substitutions: Penne rigate, mezze penne rigate, pipette, mezze maniche, sedani, rigatoni, and ziti.

RIGATONI

Big pasta tubes with ridges, normally served with chunky sauces or baked in casseroles.

Substitutions: Penne, elicoidali, paccheri, ziti and elbow macaroni.

GARGANELLI

A type of egg pasta characterised by a shape that resembles a small, ridged, rolled tube, similar to a quill.
Substitutions: Penne.

MILLERIGHE

Finely ridged, hollow pasta good with rich meat sauces and heavy cream sauces.

ANELLI

Small rings of pasta that are used in various soups and are also suitable for salads. A smaller version of the pasta is known as anellini.
Substitutions: Ditali, ditalini and tubetti.

LISLIO PICCOLO
As the name suggests, small pasta; similar to stortelli.

STORTELLI
A small hollow spiral pasta good for most ragù-style sauces, salads and soups.

FUSILLI CASARECCE
With a name that translates as 'homemade', fusilli casarecce are ¾in (20mm) wide strips of pasta about 1in (25mm) long that are loosely rolled up around their long axes. They work nicely with chunky sauces.
Substitutions: Fusilli and butterflies.

GEMELLI

A pasta variety that consists of two short pasta strands that are twisted together into a spiral shape. It is often used in casseroles and salads.

Substitutions: Fusilli, farfalle, macaroni, penne, rigatoni and ziti.

FUSILLI FATTI A MANO

A short ribbon of pasta twisted into a shape resembling a corkscrew. Fusilli is best when it is boiled and served with a thick, heavy sauce.

Substitutions: Farfalle, gemelli, macaroni, penne, rigatoni and ziti.

TROFIE

Pieces of pasta that have been rolled on a flat surface until they form a rounded length of pasta that has tapered ends. It is then twisted into its final shape

SPIRAL PASTA

Also called 'fusilli', this pasta is great served with substantial meat sauces, as the sauce becomes trapped in the coils or twists.

BUCCOLI

Can be used as an elegant-looking alternative to fusilli and is also a good pasta served cold in a salad.

RADIATORI MARCHIGIANI

Radiators or short pasta. Suitable for vegetable or meat sauces.

MARGHERITE
A pasta that has an appearance similar to a shell pasta with ridges.
Substitutions: Conchiglie and gigli.

ORECCHIETTE
Its name means 'little ears', which is exactly what this pasta looks like. It's made without eggs and tends to have a chewier and firmer texture than other pastas.

COLOURED ORECCHIETTE
One of the classic pasta shapes from Puglia, it has by now become commonplace. It is especially renowned as being an accompaniment for broccoli rabe.

FARFALLE

A pasta variety that is shaped like a bow tie—farfalle literally means 'butterfly'. It is often used in baked pasta dishes such as casseroles. It is ideal for serving with meat and vegetable sauces, as the sauce becomes trapped in the folds. A smaller version of farfalle pasta is called 'farfalline'. Substitutions: Conchiglie, fusilli and radiatori.

SHELL PASTA

Also called 'conchiglie', if large, or 'conchigliette', if smaller. The large shells are ideal for stuffing and a fish filling is often favoured because of the shape of the pasta.

SMALL SHELL PASTA

Also called 'conchigliette'. Small shells are popular in casseroles, soups and salads.

COLOURED FARFALLE
Some farfalle are coloured with spinach (green), beet juice or tomato paste (red) or squid ink (gray).

DRY SHELL GNOCCHI
Dried gnocchi is generally shaped like a hollowed shell, similar to the shape of cavatelli pasta, but with a ridged surface. Where as fresh gnocchi generally contains potatoes, the dried gnocchi contains semolina flour and no potatoes.

ROUTE/WAGON WHEEL
A wheel-shaped pasta that is also known as 'rotelle' or 'radiatore' depending on the regions.

MACARONI

Short-cut or 'elbow' macaroni, very common outside of Italy, is most often used in baked dishes and in the ever-popular macaroni and cheese.

DITALI

Small, short-cut pasta tubes that are approximately ¼in (7.5mm) long. It is often used in soups. A smaller version of ditali is known as 'ditalini'.
Substitutions: Elbow macaroni and tubetti.

FARFALLINE

A small version of farfalle, the bow-tie or butterfly-shaped pasta. It is most often used in soups.

ANELLONI
Circles of plain pasta about ¼in (7.5mm) wide and 1in (25mm) diameter. Absorbs sauces readily.

FILINI
Very thin, short-cut strands of pasta. Similar to fideos only smaller. Good in soups and liquid sauces.

MARGHERITINE
These small 'little ears' are very tasty and usually used in soup.
Substitutions: Gigli and conchiglie.

STELLINE

Tiny star-shaped pasta which adds a decorative look to soups, salads and side dishes. Stelline is a smaller version of stelle pasta. Also spelled 'stellini'.

SEME ORZO

Machine-cut pasta in melon-seed shape.

Techniques

COOKING PASTA

Cook pasta in a large, deep saucepan of water: the general rule is 4 cups water to 3½oz (100g) pasta. Bring the water to a rolling boil, toss in salt to taste (in Italy, 1 tablespoon per every 3½oz (100g) is usual), then stir in the pasta. If you wish, add some oil. When the water comes back to the boil, begin timing. The pasta is done when it's al dente, that is tender but with resistance to the bite. Remove the pasta from the water by straining it through a colander or lifting it out of the saucepan with tongs or a fork. You'll find that the pasta quantities used in this book are fairly generous. In many cases, all you'll need to make a complete meal is a tossed green or vegetable salad and some crusty bread or rolls.

BASIC EGG DOUGH

1½ cups plain flour
1 egg
1 teaspoon salt
1 tablespoon olive oil

1. Mix the flour and salt in a bowl until blended. Then, make a well in the centre. Add oil and egg into the centre until all ingredients combine thoroughly.

2. If using a food processor, process all ingredients for about 30 seconds. If the mixture forms a ball immediately and is wet to the touch, mix in more flour by the tablespoon until the dough feels soft but not sticky. If the mixture is too dry to work with, blend in water by the teaspoon until the dough just forms a ball.

3. If you have a pasta machine, the dough may be immediately kneaded and rolled out. If not, it may be better to wrap dough in plastic film and allow it to rest for about 15–30 minutes before rolling out.

ADJUSTING FLOUR AND LIQUID IN DOUGH

The moisture content of pasta dough is affected by a number of variables, including the type of wheat used, the age of the flour, its moisture content and the degree of humidity in the air. For this reason, even when you measure the ingredients very carefully, you may need to adjust the proportions of flour and liquid if the dough seems too sticky or too dry to handle.

Also, keep in mind that dough for filled pasta varieties will need to be more moist than dough for flat or tubular pasta. Add flour and water (no more than ½ teaspoon water or 1 tablespoon flour) at a time as necessary, until the dough is the proper consistency for rolling, cutting or shaping.

DESIGNER DOUGHS

Using basic egg dough as a foundation, you can add different ingredients to create your own 'designer' pastas with exciting colours and flavours. Experiment to your heart's content. Just remember that the colour and flavour of the pasta you make should complement whatever sauce you plan to serve with it. Depending on which of the following ingredients you add, you may need to adjust the proportions of liquid and flour to form a dough of proper consistency.

- Puréed vegetables: cooked beet, roasted red, green or yellow capsicum, cooked pumpkin
- Fresh puréed garlic
- Spices and seasonings: black pepper, cayenne pepper, cinnamon, chilli powder, curry, nutmeg, saffron
- Fresh or dried black olives, finely chopped
- Fresh or canned hot chillies, finely chopped

MAKING PASTA BY HAND

Machines are convenient for making pasta, but they're not essential. With only a bowl, a fork and a rolling pin, you can turn out professional-quality fresh pasta in 10 minutes.

1. Make a ring of flour blended with salt on a clean work surface. Place a beaten egg and oil in the centre of the well. Use a fork or your fingertips to incorporate the flour into the beaten egg so as to form a firm dough. On a flour-dusted work surface, knead the dough until it's smooth and cohesive (5–8 minutes). Cover with a damp cloth for 15 minutes.

2. Lightly flour your work surface. Begin with one-third of the dough at a time. Starting from the centre and moving to the edge, roll the pasta using as few strokes as possible. If the dough becomes too elastic, cover it for a few minutes with a damp cloth to prevent it from drying out. Roll it out about $1/8$in (1–2mm) thick.

3. Lightly flour the dough and roll it into a sponge-roll shape. Cut it by hand to desired thickness for flat shapes (such as linguine, fettuccine or lasagna). Dry it for 10–15 minutes on a pasta rack before cooking.

MAKING RAVIOLI

Ravioli can be made with a variety of doughs and fillings. Use the basic egg dough (see page 28) or your favourite flavoured dough recipe. The dough and filling should be compatible in flavour and colour.

Using a mould to form the ravioli simplifies the process, but it's not essential. Ravioli can be prepared ahead of serving time. After cooking, ravioli can be added to broth or your favourite sauce.

1. Roll the pasta dough into thin sheets. Place mounds of filling, about ¾ teaspoon each, at regular intervals along the length of the pasta. Brush lightly with cold water between the mounds.

2. Place another sheet of pasta over the first and use your fingers to press the sheets together between the mounds of filling.

3. Cut the ravioli with a pizza cutter or a pastry wheel. Use a fork to crimp and seal the edges.

MAKING TORTELLINI

Tortellini can be made with a variety of fillings, including the pumpkin filling shown here. It can be formed a few hours ahead and spread on lightly floured baking sheets (make sure they don't touch). Cover and refrigerate before cooking. To freeze tortellini for up to 3 months, place it in a zip-lock plastic bag in your freezer.

1. The dough should be quite thin. Cut 2in (5cm) circles from the dough. Put a teaspoon of filling in the centre of each. Brush the edges lightly with cold water.

2. Fold the circle in half to enclose the filling. Press the edges firmly to seal.

3. With the sealed edge out, place the folded circle over the index finger. Bring the ends toward each other under the finger, turning the sealed outer edge up to form a cuff. Pinch the ends together firmly. Let them dry for a few minutes on a lightly floured surface before cooking.

soups & appetizers

Mixed bean & lislio piccolo soup

SERVES 4

3oz (90g) dried red kidney beans
3oz (90g) dried cannellini beans
2 tablespoons olive oil
2oz (60g) bacon, chopped
1 onion, chopped
1 clove garlic, crushed
3 sticks celery, sliced
2 carrots, chopped
2 potatoes, chopped
6 cups chicken or vegetable stock
15oz (440g) canned tomatoes,
*   undrained and mashed*
¼ cabbage, finely shredded
2oz (60g) lislio piccolo or other
*   small pasta*
1 teaspoon dried mixed herbs
freshly ground black pepper
freshly grated Parmesan cheese
*   to serve*
basil leaves to garnish

1. Place red kidney and cannellini beans in a bowl. Cover with cold water and set aside to soak overnight. Drain when ready to use.

2. Heat the oil in a saucepan over a medium heat. Add bacon, onion and garlic and cook, stirring, for 5 minutes or until onion is tender. Add celery, carrots and potatoes and cook for 1 minute longer.

3. Stir in stock, tomatoes, cabbage, pasta, red kidney and cannellini beans, herbs and black pepper to taste. Bring to the boil. Boil for 10 minutes, then reduce heat and simmer, stirring occasionally, for 1 hour or until beans are tender. Sprinkle with Parmesan and serve garnished with basil leaves.

NOTE
Extra vegetables of your choice may be added—it is a good way to use up vegetable leftovers.

Minestrone

1. Place the stock, tomatoes, wine, onions, carrots, turnip, celery and bell peppers in a large saucepan. Bring to the boil, reduce the heat and simmer for 20 minutes.

2. Add the courgette, kidney beans, penne and turmeric. Simmer for a further 40 minutes, stirring regularly, until the vegetables are tender. Season with salt and pepper.

3. To make the pesto place the basil, garlic and Parmesan in a food processor or blender. Blend until finely chopped. While the motor is running, gradually add the olive oil through the feed tube until a paste is formed. Season with salt and pepper. Serve the soup in large soup bowls, topped with 1 tablespoon of pesto and basil leaves.

4¼ cups chicken stock
15oz (440g) canned peeled
    tomatoes, chopped
2 cups dry white wine
2 onions, diced
3 carrots, diced
1 turnip, diced
2 sticks celery, sliced
2 red bell peppers (capsicums), diced
1 large courgette (zucchini), sliced
15oz (440g) canned red kidney
    beans, drained
¾ cup penne
½ teaspoon ground turmeric
salt and freshly ground black pepper

PESTO
1 bunch fresh basil, handful of leaves
    kept aside to garnish
3 cloves garlic, crushed
2oz (60g) Parmesan cheese,
    finely grated
½ cup olive oil
salt and freshly ground black pepper

Spagetti & broccoli soup

SERVES 4

3½oz (100g) spaghetti
2½oz (75g) butter
1 clove garlic, crushed
1 large onion, roughly chopped
2 rashers bacon, chopped
2lb 4oz (1kg) broccoli, cut into florets
7oz (200g) courgette (zucchini),
    chopped into rounds
2 tablespoons chopped fresh parsley
52fl oz (1½ litres) chicken stock
salt to taste
freshly ground black pepper
freshly grated Parmesan cheese to
    serve
fresh parsley to garnish

1. Cook the spaghetti in a large pot of rapidly boiling salted water until tender but still firm to the bite. Drain well and set aside.

2. Heat butter in a large soup pot and lightly brown garlic, onion and bacon.

3. Add broccoli and sauté quickly for 2–3 minutes. Add courgette, parsley, chicken stock, salt and pepper. Bring to the boil and allow to simmer until broccoli is cooked (approximately 20 minutes).

4. At the last minute, add spaghetti and heat through. Serve with generous quantities of Parmesan and finely chopped parsley.

French vegetable soup with pistou

SERVES 4–6

1. Place beans in a bowl. Cover with cold water and set aside to soak overnight. Drain, then place in a pan with fresh water to cover. Bring to the boil, cover and simmer gently for 15 minutes. Drain.

2. Melt the butter in a large deep pan and sauté the vegetables, including the beans, until softened for about 5 minutes. Cover with cold water and add salt. Cover and simmer gently for 1 hour.

3. Add the farfalle to the soup, cooking for a further 15 minutes.

4. Make pistou by processing the basil with the garlic in a food processor or blender. Add the tomato, tomato paste and cheese. Purée to a paste, adding oil gradually through the feed tube. Stir the pistou into the soup just before serving. Serve piping hot with crusty bread.

17½oz (500g) dried borlotti or
    navy beans
1oz (30g) butter
1 large onion, finely chopped
17½oz (500g) green beans, trimmed
17½oz (500g) courgette (zucchini)
    or squash, cut into ⅛in- (5mm)
    thick slices
6 medium potatoes, cut into ¼in
    (1cm) cubes
101½fl oz (3½ litres) water
1–2 teaspoons salt (the amount
    of vegetables calls for a good
    seasoning)
2oz (60g) farfalle

PISTOU
1 cup fresh basil leaves
4 cloves garlic, crushed
1 large tomato, peeled and chopped
1 tablespoon tomato paste
½ cup grated Parmesan or Gruyère
    cheese
3 tablespoons olive oil

Sweet potato, ditalini & leek soup

SERVES 6

2 teaspoons canola oil
2 leeks, thinly sliced
pinch saffron
2lb 4oz (1kg) sweet potato, peeled
    and chopped
36fl oz (1 litre) reduced-salt chicken
    stock
1 cinnamon stick
1 bouquet garni
3½oz (100g) ditalini
2 tablespoons chopped fresh chives
    to garnish

LAVASH CRISPS
2 sheets lavash bread
1 tablespoon olive oil
2 tablespoons finely grated
    Parmesan cheese

1. Heat the oil in a large pot, add the leeks and cook over a medium heat for 5 minutes or until the leeks are soft and golden. Add the saffron and sweet potato and stir for about 5 minutes or until the sweet potato begins to soften.

2. Stir in the stock, cinnamon stick and bouquet garni. Bring to the boil then reduce the heat and simmer for 30 minutes or until the sweet potato is very soft. Remove the cinnamon stick and bouquet garni.

3. Cook the ditalini in a large pot of rapidly boiling salted water until tender but still firm to the bite. Drain well.

4. Purée the soup in batches until smooth then return to the pot along with the pasta and reheat gently. If it is too thick add a little water.

5. To make lavash crisps use a star-shaped cookie cutter to cut out shapes from the bread, brush lightly with oil, sprinkle with Parmesan and place another star on top. Grill until crisp and golden.

6. To serve, ladle the soup into bowls, float lavash stars on top and sprinkle with chives.

Individual macaroni, broccolini & cauliflower cheese

SERVES 4

1. Preheat the oven to 400°F (200°C). Lightly grease four 9fl oz (250ml) ramekins.

2. Cook the macaroni in a large pot of rapidly boiling salted water until tender but still firm to the bite. Drain well and set aside.

3. Steam or microwave the cauliflower and broccolini or broccoli separately until tender. Rinse under cold water and drain well.

4. Heat the canola spread in a small pot, add the flour, saffron and nutmeg and cook, stirring constantly, until bubbling. Remove from the heat and gradually stir in the milk.

5. Return the pot to the heat and bring to the boil, stirring constantly until the sauce boils and thickens. Reduce the heat and simmer for 5 minutes.

6. Put the macaroni in the base of the ramekins, top with cauliflower and broccolini and pour over the sauce. Sprinkle with cheese. Bake for 15 minutes or until the sauce is golden and bubbling.

2oz (60g) macaroni
8½oz (250g) cauliflower, cut into florets
8½oz (250g) broccolini or broccoli, cut into florets
1oz (30g) canola spread
1 tablespoon plain flour
pinch saffron
pinch nutmeg
8½fl oz (250ml) reduced-fat evaporated milk
⅓ cup grated reduced-fat Cheddar cheese

Baked farfalle with turkey

SERVES 6

canola cooking spray
7oz (200g) farfalle
3½oz (100g) baby spinach leaves,
   washed
7oz (200g) shaved light turkey
   breast
6 eggs, lightly beaten
½ cup low- or reduced-fat milk
⅓ cup grated reduced-fat
   Cheddar cheese
2 tablespoons cranberry sauce

1. Preheat the oven to 350°F (180°C). Spray six large 9fl oz (250ml) muffin tins with canola spray and line the bases with baking paper.

2. Cook the farfalle in a large pot of rapidly boiling salted water until just tender. Drain well.

3. Line the bases and sides of the muffin tins with the farfalle. Steam the spinach until it wilts, drain well and squeeze out any excess moisture.

4. Fill the centre of each muffin tin with turkey breast and spinach.

5. Whisk together the eggs, milk and cheese and pour into the muffin tins. Top with a spoonful of cranberry sauce. Bake for 20 minutes or until set. Turn out and serve with a green salad.

Tomatoes stuffed with margheritine & arugula

SERVES 4

1. Slice the top off each tomato and scoop out the seeds and flesh. Sprinkle the inside with salt and leave to drain, cut-side down, on absorbent paper for 1 hour.

2. Cook the pasta in plenty of boiling salted water until tender but still firm to the bite, then drain. Add the arugula and 2 tablespoons of the oil.

3. Heat the remaining oil in a frying pan and cook the garlic, chillies and anchovies for 2 minutes or until the anchovies have disintegrated. Add to the pasta and arugula, pour in the vinegar and mix well. Fill the tomatoes with the pasta mixture. Serve warm.

NOTE
Even people who don't like anchovies will love this dish. They melt away during cooking but give the pasta extra flavour, together with the arugula and balsamic vinegar.

4 large ripe but firm tomatoes
salt
1 cup margheritine
1 cup shredded arugula (rocket)
6 tablespoons extra virgin olive oil
2 cloves garlic, sliced
½ teapoon crushed dried chillies
4 anchovy fillets, drained
1 tablespoon balsamic vinegar

Cannelloni with crab & endive

SERVES 6

12 large cannelloni tubes
oil for frying
24oz (750g) crabmeat
8½oz (250g) mayonnaise
freshly ground black pepper
2 tablespoons freshly squeezed
*   lemon juice*
paprika
1 head curly endive
8½oz (250g) cherry tomatoes

1. Preheat the oven to 350°F (180°C). Cook the cannelloni in boiling salted water until tender but still firm to the bite. Drain and cool.

2. Sauté the cannelloni in hot oil for 5 minutes until crisp. Remove and drain on absorbent paper.

3. Combine the crabmeat, mayonnaise, pepper to taste and lemon juice and spoon into the cannelloni tubes. Place the filled cannelloni tubes in a shallow ovenproof dish, sprinkle with paprika and bake for 15 minutes or until heated through.

4. Serve with the curly endive and cherry tomatoes.

Vegetable lasagne stacks with pesto

1. To make the pesto put the garlic, pine nuts, basil leaves and Parmesan in a food processor and process until coarsely chopped. With the motor running, gradually add the oil and process until the mixture becomes a smooth paste.

2. Cut the lasagne sheets into twelve 3¼in (8cm) squares. Cook in a large pot of rapidly boiling salted water until tender but still firm to the bite. Drain well.

3. Put one sheet in the centre of each plate, top each with a couple of spinach leaves, a slice each of tomato and bocconcini, a fresh basil leaf and a spoonful of pesto.

4. Top with another sheet of lasagne and layer as before, finishing with a layer of lasagne. Each stack should have two complete layers.

5. Place a generous spoonful of pesto on top of each stack and serve immediately.

13oz (375g) fresh lasagne sheets
2oz (60g) baby spinach leaves
4 large vine-ripened tomatoes, cut
*   into thick slices*
6 large bocconcini, cut into
*   thick slices*
8 fresh basil leaves

PESTO
2 cloves garlic
2 tablespoons pine nuts, toasted
1 cup fresh basil leaves
2 tablespoons finely grated
*   Parmesan cheese*
2 tablespoons extra virgin olive oil

cheese & egg

Tagliatelle with squash & ricotta

SERVES 4

6 tablespoons butter
1 onion, very finely chopped
17½oz (500g) butternut squash,
    peeled and cut into thin slices
½ cup milk
8½oz (250g) ricotta cheese
½ teaspoon freshly grated nutmeg
salt and freshly ground black pepper
17½oz (500g) fresh tagliatelle
2 tablespoons poppy seeds
freshly grated Parmesan cheese
    to serve

1. Heat the butter in a large, heavy-based saucepan. Add the onion and cook gently, covered, for 5 minutes or until the onion has softened but not browned. Add the squash and cook for 5 minutes, stirring occasionally, until slightly softened. Stir in 2 tablespoons of the milk, then simmer, uncovered, for 20 minutes, adding more milk, a little at a time, until it has all been added and the squash is tender.

2. Mash the ricotta with the nutmeg and pepper in a bowl. Cook the pasta in plenty of boiling salted water until tender but still firm to the bite. Drain, reserving 1 cup of the cooking water, then mix the pasta with the squash mixture.

3. Stir a little of the reserved pasta water into the seasoned ricotta until it's the consistency of heavy cream. Place the tagliatelle on warmed plates, spoon over the ricotta and sprinkle with poppy seeds. Serve with plenty of Parmesan.

NOTE
Simplicity is the key to this unusual dish. Tagliatelle and butternut squash are topped with nutmeg-flavoured ricotta and a generous sprinkling of poppy seeds.

Rigatoni with mascarpone, tomato & basil

SERVES 4

1. Place the tomatoes in a bowl and pour boiling water over. Leave for 30 seconds, then peel, deseed and chop. Heat the butter in a large, heavy-based skillet, then add the garlic. Cook for 1 minute to soften. Add the tomatoes and cook for 2–3 minutes or until softened, stirring occasionally.

2. Add the tomato sauce to the tomatoes, cook for 2 minutes, then stir in the mascarpone and bring to the boil. Add the chilli powder and salt to taste.

3. Transfer the sauce to a bowl, add the basil and keep warm. Cook the pasta in plenty of boiling salted water until tender but still firm to the bite, then drain. Spoon the pasta into the bowl, toss thoroughly, then sprinkle over the Parmesan. Serve with extra Parmesan.

NOTE
The sauce for this pasta is very easy to make, and the tomatoes, coupled with the creamy mascarpone, produce a great result. You can use penne instead of rigatoni.

17½oz (500g) ripe tomatoes
2oz (60g) unsalted butter
1 clove garlic, crushed
2 tablespoons tomato sauce
5 tablespoons mascarpone
½ teaspoon chilli powder
salt
12 fresh basil leaves, torn
14oz (400g) rigatoni
6 tablespoons freshly grated
*   Parmesan cheese, plus extra*
*   to serve*

Lobster alfredo

1 tablespoon butter
½ cup lobster bouillon or fish
  bouillon
2 cups heavy cream
1¼ cups freshly grated Parmesan
  cheese
1 dash Worcestershire sauce
¼ teaspoon Tabasco sauce
¼ teaspoon freshly ground black
  pepper
1 teaspoon Dijon mustard
12oz (350g) mafaldine
1 cup freshly shucked lobster meat
4 egg yolks
¼ cup chopped fresh parsley

1. In a medium-size saucepan, over a medium heat, melt the butter and add the lobster bouillon and cream and turn the heat up to medium-high.

2. When the cream is hot, just before boiling, add the Parmesan and whisk briskly until all the cheese is melted and dissolved into the cream. Add the Worcestershire, Tabasco, black pepper and Dijon mustard and whisk thoroughly again. Reduce the heat to a fast simmer and allow the mixture to simmer for 20 minutes.

3. While the sauce is simmering, cook the pasta in plenty of boiling salted water until tender but still firm to the bite, drain and set onto plates. Cut the lobster meat into small pieces and add to the sauce. Add the egg yolks and turn the heat to medium-high. The sauce should be of medium thickness. Ladle the sauce over the pasta, sprinkle with freshly chopped parsley and serve.

Lasagne with spinach, ricotta & fontina

SERVES 4

1. Preheat the oven to 400°F (200°C). Rinse spinach and place in a saucepan with water still clinging to its leaves. Cover and cook for 5 minutes or until wilted. Drain, refresh under cold water, then squeeze out all excess liquid. Chop finely. Cook lasagne in plenty of boiling salted water until tender but still firm to the bite. Drain, and pat dry with absorbent paper.

2. Brush a 2 x 8in (30 x 20cm) ovenproof dish with a little of the melted butter. In a bowl, combine spinach, Fontina or Gruyère, Parmesan, ricotta, crème fraîche, nutmeg, salt and pepper.

3. Cover base of the dish with a layer of lasagne sheets and spread over 3 tablespoons of the spinach mixture. Repeat the layering until all the lasagne is used, making no more than 6 layers. Finish with the remaining spinach mixture. Drizzle with the remaining melted butter, then cook for 20–30 minutes or until golden brown.

NOTE
Layers of creamy cheese, pasta and lots of fresh spinach make a delicious alternative to traditional meat lasagne. Let the dish rest for a few minutes before serving.

17½oz (500g) fresh spinach
6oz (170g) dried lasagne sheets
2oz (60g) unsalted butter, melted
1½oz (45g) Fontina or Gruyère
  cheese, coarsely grated
1½oz (45g) Parmesan cheese, grated
8½oz (250g) ricotta cheese
5fl oz (145ml) crème fraîche
freshly grated nutmeg
salt and freshly ground black pepper

Penne with goat's cheese & asparagus

SERVES 4

1 tablespoon sunflower oil
2 tablespoons butter
2 red onions, thinly sliced
1 clove garlic, finely chopped
17½oz (500g) penne
8½oz (250g) fresh asparagus,
  trimmed and cut into pieces
1 cup peas, fresh or frozen
2 cups goat's cheese, roughly
  crumbled
freshly ground black pepper

1. Heat the oil and butter in a skillet and cook onion over a medium heat for 7 minutes, stirring occasionally. Add the garlic and cook for a further 3 minutes or until the onions are golden and crisp.

2. Meanwhile, bring a large saucepan of salted water to the boil. Add the pasta and cook for 5 minutes. Add the asparagus and cook for a further 2 minutes, then add the peas and cook for 2 minutes. When cooked, drain well.

3. Return the pasta and vegetables to the saucepan and gently stir through nearly all the onions, saving a small amount for the garnish. Add cheese and plenty of pepper and mix together well. Serve topped with the remaining crispy onions.

NOTE
The crispy onions, melting goat's cheese and delicate asparagus spears go together beautifully in this fast and fashionable pasta dish.

Whole-wheat spaghetti with four cheeses

SERVES 4

1. Preheat the oven to 400°F (200°C). Cook the pasta in plenty of boiling salted water until tender but still firm to the bite, then drain. Return to the saucepan and toss with ½ the butter and ½ the Parmesan. Add the Gruyère, Bel Paese, mozzarella and plenty of pepper, then mix well.

2. Transfer the pasta and cheese mixture to a buttered ovenproof dish. Level the top and dot with the remaining butter. Sprinkle with the rest of the Parmesan. Bake for 10–15 minutes or until the top is crisp and golden. Leave to stand for 5 minutes before serving.

NOTE

This mixture of hard and soft cheeses is baked until it melts into the spaghetti. It's quite rich and very filling, so follow it with a light fruity pudding.Bel Paese cheese is from the Lombardy region of Italy. It is a modern, semi-soft, creamy cheese that is matured for 6–8 weeks. Ivory in color, it has a delicate, sweet flavor and a light, milky aroma. The genuine Italian article can be identified by its wrapping, which features an image of a priest and the map of Italy. The name means 'beautiful land' and was inspired by the title of a book by Stoppani. Bel Paese is very similar to French St. Paulin. It can also be used instead of mozzarella.

13oz (375g) dried whole-wheat spaghetti
6 tablespoons butter
4 tablespoons freshly grated Parmesan cheese
⅓ cup Gruyère cheese, cut into matchsticks
⅓ cup Bel Paese cheese, cut into matchsticks
½ cup mozzarella cheese, cut into pieces
salt and freshly ground black pepper

Shell gnocchi with oysters

SERVES 4

8½oz (250g) medium shell gnocchi
1 tablespoon olive or vegetable oil
3 cloves garlic, chopped
4oz (125g) select oysters or
    12 oysters, shucked, with liquid
    reserved or 4oz (125g) bottle
    oysters with juice
3 tablespoons dry white wine
¼ cup clam juice
3 tablespoons evaporated skim milk
8½oz (250g) fresh spinach, washed,
    hard stems removed
6 fresh basil leaves, chopped
½ cup chopped fresh parsley
salt and white pepper

1. Cook the pasta in plenty of boiling salted water until tender but still firm to the bite. While the pasta is cooking, heat the oil in a non-stick skillet and sauté the garlic carefully to avoid burning. Add the oysters and pour the white wine over. Bring to the boil. Add the clam juice, oyster juice and the evaporated milk, bring back to boiling and cook for 3 more minutes. Add the spinach to the skillet and cook until wilted.

2. When the pasta is done, drain and combine with the oyster and spinach mixture. Add the basil, parsley and salt and pepper to taste. Serve immediately.

Penne with bell peppers & mascarpone

SERVES 4

1. Heat the oil in a large skillet and fry the garlic, onions and peppers for 10 minutes or until the vegetables have softened, stirring frequently. Meanwhile, cook the pasta in plenty of boiling salted water until tender but still firm to the bite.

2. Stir ½ the mascarpone, lemon juice, parsley and pepper into the bell pepper mixture. Cook for 5 minutes or until the mascarpone has melted.

3. Drain the pasta and stir in the remaining mascarpone, then add to the bell pepper mixture, tossing together well. Serve with a sprinkling of Parmesan (if using).

NOTE

Soft mascarpone cheese gives this colorful dish a particularly luscious texture and taste, but cream cheese or ricotta make good substitutes. Serve it with warmed ciabatta.

2 tablespoons olive oil
1 clove garlic, crushed
2 red onions, chopped
1 red, 1 yellow and 1 green bell pepper (capsicum), deseeded and cut into ½in (1cm) pieces
3½ cups penne
8½oz (250g) mascarpone cheese
juice of ½ lemon
4 tablespoons chopped fresh parsley
freshly ground black pepper
4 tablespoons grated Parmesan cheese (optional)

Traditional lasagne

SERVES 6

24 sheets instant lasagne*
2oz (60g) mozzarella cheese, grated

CHEESE SAUCE
2½oz (75g) butter
⅓ cup all-purpose (plain) flour
2 cups milk
*3oz (90g) tasty cheese (aged
    Cheddar), grated*
freshly ground black pepper

MEAT SAUCE
2 teaspoons vegetable oil
2 onions, chopped
2 cloves garlic, crushed
2lb 12oz (1.25kg) ground beef
*2 x 15oz (440g) canned diced
    tomatoes*
¾ cup red wine
2 tablespoons chopped mixed herbs
freshly ground black pepper

*no pre-cooking required

1. To make cheese sauce, melt butter in a saucepan over a medium heat. Stir in flour and cook, stirring, for 1 minute. Remove pan from heat and whisk in milk. Return pan to heat and cook, stirring, for 4–5 minutes or until sauce boils and thickens. Stir in cheese and black pepper to taste and set aside.

2. Preheat the oven to 350°F (180°C). To make meat sauce, heat oil in a skillet over a medium heat. Add onions and garlic and cook, stirring, for 3 minutes or until onions are soft. Add beef and cook, stirring, for 5 minutes or until beef is brown. Stir in tomatoes, wine and herbs, bring to simmering point and simmer, stirring occasionally, for 15 minutes or until sauce in reduced and thickened. Season to taste with black pepper.

3. Line the base of a large greased baking dish with 6 lasagne sheets. Top with one-quarter of the meat sauce and one-quarter of the cheese sauce. Repeat layers to use all ingredients, ending with a layer of cheese sauce.

4. Sprinkle top of lasagne with mozzarella cheese and bake for 30-40 minutes or until it is hot and bubbling and the top is golden.

Tuna lasagne

1. To make the sauce, combine the milk and water and set aside. Melt the butter in a saucepan, stir in the flour and curry powder and cook for 2–3 minutes. Remove the pan from the heat and whisk in the milk mixture. Return the sauce to the heat and cook, stirring constantly, for 4–5 minutes or until the sauce boils and thickens. Remove the pan from the heat and whisk in the eggs and cheese. Season to taste with black pepper. Set aside.

2. Preheat the oven to 350°F (180°C). Melt the butter in a skillet and cook the celery and onion for 4–5 minutes or until onion is soft. Spoon a little sauce over the base of a lightly greased, shallow, ovenproof dish. Top with 3 lasagne sheets and spread over half the tuna and half the celery mixture, then a layer of sauce. Repeat layers, finishing with a layer of lasagne, then sauce.

3. Combine the cheese, curry powder and paprika, and sprinkle over the lasagne. Bake for 30–35 minutes or until the noodles are tender and the top is golden.

½oz (15g) butter
2 sticks celery, finely chopped
1 onion, chopped
9 sheets instant lasagne*
14oz (400g) canned tuna, drained
 and flaked
2 tablespoons grated tasty cheese
 (aged Cheddar)
1 teaspoon curry powder
½ teaspoon ground sweet paprika

CURRY SAUCE
2 cups milk
1 cup water
1oz (30g) butter
⅓ cup all-purpose (plain) flour
2 teaspoons curry powder
2 eggs, beaten
2 tablespoons grated tasty cheese
 (aged Cheddar)
freshly ground black pepper

*no pre-cooking required

Tuna noodle casserole

SERVES 4

8½oz (250g) macaroni
2 tablespoons butter
2 tablespoons all-purpose (plain)
  flour
1 teaspoon salt
1 cup milk
1 cup shredded aged Cheddar cheese
6oz (170g) canned tuna, drained
14oz (400g) frozen green peas
½ cup grated Cheddar cheese, extra
¼ cup grated Parmesan cheese

1. Preheat the oven to 350°F (180°C).
2. In a large pot of boiling salted water cook the noodles until tender but still firm to the bite. Drain well.
3. In a medium saucepan combine the butter, flour and salt. Stir until the butter is melted and ingredients are combined evenly.
4. Add the milk and whisk until the white sauce thickens (usually, it is at the proper consistency by the time it begins to boil). Add the cheese to the mixture and whisk until the cheese is melted and mixture is well blended.
5. Stir in the tuna and peas.
6. In a casserole dish combine the noodles and tuna mixture. Sprinkle extra Cheddar and Parmesan cheese on top and bake for 30 minutes or until the top is golden.

Fettuccine with caviar

SERVES 4

1. Cook the fettuccine in boiling water until tender but still firm to the bite, then drain.
2. Meanwhile, heat the oil in a large skillet over moderate heat. Add the garlic and cook for 2 minutes.
3. Add the cooked fettuccine, chives, red and black caviar and eggs, toss well and heat through. Top with sour cream and serve.

12oz (340g) fettuccine
4 tablespoons olive oil
2 cloves garlic, crushed
2 tablespoons snipped fresh chives
3 tablespoons red caviar
3 tablespoons black caviar
2 hard-boiled eggs, chopped
¼ cup sour cream

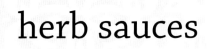

herb sauces

Pesto fettuccine

SERVES 4

17½oz (500g) fettuccine

PESTO
1 large bunch fresh basil, handful of
    leaves kept aside for garnish
½ bunch fresh parsley, broken into
    sprigs
2oz (60g) Parmesan or Romano
    cheese, grated
1oz (30g) pine nuts or almonds
2 large cloves garlic, quartered
freshly ground black pepper
4½ tablespoons olive oil

1. To make the pesto, place basil leaves, parsley, Parmesan or Romano cheese, pine nuts or almonds, garlic and pepper to taste in a food processor or blender and process to finely chop. With machine running, slowly add oil and continue processing to make a smooth paste.

2. Cook the pasta in plenty of boiling salted water until tender but still firm to the bite. Drain and divide between serving bowls, top with pesto and serve immediately, garnished with basil leaves.

NOTE
Spinach pesto makes a tasty alternative when fresh basil is unavailable. To make, use fresh spinach in place of the basil and add 1 teaspoon of dried basil.

Rigatoni with bell peppers

SERVES 6

1. In a large saucepan, heat the oil, add onions and sauté for 2 minutes.

2. Place the garlic cloves, peppers, tomatoes, chillies, oregano and several grinds of black pepper on top of the onions. Cover the saucepan with a tightly fitting lid and allow the mixture to simmer on a very low heat for 40 minutes.

3. Remove the garlic cloves and adjust seasoning by adding sugar, salt and pepper to taste.

4. Cook the pasta in plenty of boiling salted water until tender but still firm to the bite. Drain.

5. Mix half of the pepper sauce with the pasta.

6. When serving the pasta, spoon a little of the reserved sauce over the top. Garnish with Parmesan and finely chopped parsley.

½ cup olive oil
2 large onions, finely sliced
6 cloves garlic, peeled and bruised
6 large bell peppers (red, green and yellow), sliced into finger-width strips
15oz (425g) canned tomatoes
2 chillies, finely chopped
1 teaspoon oregano
½ teaspoon sugar
salt and freshly ground black pepper
17½oz (500g) rigatoni
freshly grated Parmesan cheese for garnish
finely chopped fresh parsley for garnish

Conchiglie with six-herb sauce

SERVES 6

17½oz (500g) conchiglie

SIX-HERB SAUCE
1oz (30g) butter
2 tablespoons chopped fresh
   rosemary
12 small fresh sage leaves
12 small fresh basil leaves
2 tablespoons fresh marjoram leaves
2 tablespoons fresh oregano leaves
2 tablespoons chopped fresh parsley
2 cloves garlic, chopped
¼ cup dry white wine
¼ cup vegetable bouillon

1. Cook pasta in plenty of boiling salted water until tender but still firm to the bite. Drain, set aside and keep warm.

2. To make sauce, melt butter in a saucepan over a medium heat. Add rosemary, sage, basil, marjoram, oregano, parsley and garlic and cook, stirring, for 1 minute.

3. Stir in wine and bouillon, bring to a simmer and cook for 4 minutes. To serve, spoon sauce over hot pasta and toss to combine.

Gnocchi with spinach, arugula & basil pesto

SERVES 4

1. Cook the gnocchi in a large pot of rapidly boiling water, just until they float to the surface. Remove with a slotted spoon, drain well and set aside. Keep warm.

2. Steam the spinach until it wilts, drain and squeeze out any excess moisture.

3. Put the spinach, arugula, basil, garlic, pine nuts and Parmesan in a food processor and process until smooth. With the motor running, gradually add the oil and process to form a smooth paste.

4. Spoon the pesto over the cooked gnocchi and toss to coat. Season with the pepper. Serve garnished with shaved Parmesan.

17½oz (500g) fresh potato gnocchi
2 cups baby spinach leaves, washed
2 cups baby arugula (rocket) leaves, washed
1 cup fresh basil leaves
2 cloves garlic
4 tablespoons pine nuts, toasted
¼ cup grated Parmesan cheese
2 tablespoons extra virgin olive oil
freshly ground black pepper
freshly shaved Parmesan cheese for garnish

Squid & herb spaghetti

SERVES 4

17½oz (500g) squid tubes, cleaned
and cut into rings
17½oz (500g) spaghetti or
vermicelli
2 teaspoons olive oil
1 red onion, finely diced
1 clove garlic, crushed
4 Roma tomatoes, deseeded and
diced
½ cup pitted Kalamata olives, rinsed
and drained, sliced
¼ cup low-salt chicken or fish
bouillon
¼ cup dry white wine
1 cup chopped fresh cilantro
(coriander)
3 tablespoons chopped fresh mint
freshly ground black pepper

1. Bring a large saucepan of water to the boil. Using a slotted spoon or wire basket, carefully lower squid into the water. Cook for 5–10 seconds or until it just turns white and is firm. Drain. Plunge into iced water. Drain again. Set aside.

2. Bring a large saucepan of fresh, salted water to the boil. Add the pasta and cook until tender but still firm to the bite. Drain.

3. Meanwhile, place the oil, onion and garlic in a non-stick skillet over a medium heat. Cook, stirring, for 3–4 minutes or until the onion is soft. Add tomatoes, olives, bouillon and wine. Bring to a simmer. Simmer for 5 minutes. Stir in the cilantro, mint, squid and pepper to taste. Cook for 1–2 minutes or until heated through.

4. Drain the pasta. Add squid mixture. Toss to combine.

Smoked salmon ravioli with lemon dill sauce

SERVES 4

1. Place the salmon, 1 tablespoon of the egg white, the cream and dill in a food processor, and process until well combined, like a mousse.

2. Sprinkle the cornstarch on a bench and lay the won ton skins in rows of four.

3. Brush every second skin around the edge with remaining egg white. On alternate skins, place a teaspoon of mixture in the middle. Lay the other skin on top, gently pinch around the mixture, so they look like pillows or rounds.

4. Half-fill a large saucepan with water and the oil and bring to the boil. Add 2–3 pieces of ravioli at a time and cook for 2–3 minutes. Remove from water with a slotted spoon, set aside and cover with cling wrap.

5. For the lemon dill sauce, melt the butter in a saucepan, add the flour, and cook for 1 minute. Add the wine, stir until smooth, then add the cream and lemon juice. Bring to the boil and reduce until the sauce is a pouring consistency.

6. To serve, add the dill and salt and pepper to the sauce and pour over the ravioli.

4oz (125g) smoked salmon
1 egg white
1½ tablespoons cream
2 teaspoons roughly chopped
    fresh dill
2–3 tablespoons cornstarch
    (cornflour)
fresh pasta dough roll out very thin
    (recipe on page 28) or 32 wonton
    skins
1 teaspoon oil

LEMON DILL SAUCE
1 tablespoon butter
1 tablespoon all-purpose (plain) flour
¾ cup dry white wine
¾ cup heavy cream
½ lemon juice
2 tablespoons roughly chopped
    fresh dill
salt and freshly ground black pepper

Tricolor gnocchi with fresh herbs

SERVES 4

10½oz (300g) tricolor gnocchi
3½oz (100g) butter
1 clove garlic, chopped
2 tablespoons fresh thyme
2 tablespoons chopped fresh parsley
1 teaspoon fresh oregano
1 small bunch fresh basil, chopped
1 red bell pepper (capsicum), sliced
*   into thin strips*
freshly grated Parmesan cheese
*   to serve*
6 sun-dried tomatoes, finely sliced
*   for garnish*

1. Place gnocchi into boiling salted water and remove with slotted spoon after approximately 1 minute or when gnocchi rise to surface. Drain.

2. Melt butter in a skillet. Add garlic and herbs and fry for 1 minute on high heat, shaking pan continuously. Add gnocchi and bell pepper and sauté until gnocchi are golden brown and well coated with herbs. Serve with grated Parmesan and sliced sun-dried tomatoes.

Papparadelle with rosemary butter sauce

1. Place the garlic and rosemary in a small saucepan with the butter. Cook over a low heat, stirring often, for 4 minutes or until the butter has melted and browned and the garlic has softened. Crumble the bouillon cube into the mixture and stir until completely dissolved.

2. Cook the pasta in plenty of boiling salted water until tender but still firm to the bite. Add 2 tablespoons of cooking water to the butter sauce. Drain the pasta, transfer it to a warmed serving bowl, pour the sauce over and toss well. Serve with plenty of Parmesan.

NOTE

The sauce for this pasta is incredibly quick and easy and the rosemary and fried garlic give it plenty of flavor. Be sure to use a quality bouillon cube.

4 cloves garlic, finely chopped
1 tablespoon finely chopped
 fresh rosemary
6 tablespoons butter, cubed
1 beef bouillon cube
17½oz (500g) fresh pappardelle
freshly grated Parmesan cheese
 to serve

Cavatelli with arugula, hot pancetta & sun-dried tomatoes

SERVES 4

17½oz (500g) cavatelli
1 tablespoon extra virgin olive oil
2 cloves garlic, crushed
3½oz (100g) sliced hot pancetta,
    roughly chopped
1 cup Italian tomato sauce
3½oz (100g) sliced semi sun-dried
    tomatoes
1 bunch arugula (rocket), washed
    and drained
salt and freshly ground black pepper

1. Cook pasta in plenty of boiling salted water until tender but still firm to the bite. Drain and set aside.

2. Heat oil in a saucepan, add garlic and pancetta and cook for 2 minutes or until garlic is soft and flavors are well combined.

3. Add the pasta, tomato sauce, semi sun-dried tomatoes, arugula and salt and pepper to the pan, and heat through. Toss sauce through pasta and serve.

vegetable sauces

Fettuccine with leeks

SERVES 4

17½oz (500g) fettuccine
2oz (60g) butter
2 large leeks, halved, well washed
  and thinly sliced
7oz (200g) ham slices, cut into strips
1 red bell pepper (capsicum), cut into
  strips
1 cup heavy cream
freshly ground black pepper
fresh parsley sprigs for garnish

1. Cook fettuccine in boiling salted water in a large saucepan until tender but still firm to the bite. Drain, set aside and keep warm.

2. Heat butter in a large skillet and cook leeks for 8–10 minutes or until tender. Add ham and bell pepper and cook for 2–3 minutes longer. Stir in cream, bring to the boil, then reduce heat and simmer for 4–5 minutes.

3. Add fettuccine to pan and toss to combine. Season with black pepper (to taste) and serve immediately, garnished with a sprig of parsley.

Penne with cannellini bean purée

SERVES 4

1. Preheat the oven to 285°F (140°C). Place the cannellini beans, garlic and parsley in a food processor. Process or hand blend until smooth, drizzling in the Worcestershire sauce and oil as you blend. Pour in enough of the reserved bean liquid to thin the sauce to the consistency of thin heavy cream. Season and transfer to an ovenproof bowl, then place in the oven to warm through while the pasta is cooking.

2. Cook the pasta in plenty of boiling salted water until tender but still firm to the bite, then drain. Transfer to the bowl with the bean mixture and toss well. Garnish with basil and serve with Parmesan.

NOTE
Cannellini beans are grown almost exclusively in Italy. The small, dried white beans make a delicious purée when flavoured with parsley, basil and Parmesan.

14oz (400g) canned cannellini beans, drained, with liquid reserved
1 clove garlic, quartered
2 tablespoons chopped Italian parsley
½ teaspoon Worcestershire sauce
3½fl oz (100ml) olive oil
salt and freshly ground black pepper
12oz (340g) penne
12 fresh basil leaves, torn, for garnish
freshly grated Parmesan cheese to serve

Penne with double tomato sauce

SERVES 4

1 tablespoon extra virgin olive oil
1 red onion, finely chopped
2 sticks celery, finely chopped
2 cups canned chopped tomatoes
1 tablespoon tomato paste
1½ cups vegetable bouillon
1 cup cherry tomatoes, halved
1 teaspoon golden sugar
sea salt and freshly ground
   black pepper
1½ cups penne
4 tablespoons crème fraîche
   (optional)

1. Heat the oil in a large, heavy-based saucepan. Add the red onion and celery and cook, uncovered, for 5 minutes over a medium heat until the vegetables are tender. Add the chopped tomatoes, tomato paste and bouillon and bring to the boil. Simmer, uncovered, for 15 minutes, stirring occasionally, until reduced and thickened.

2. Add the cherry tomatoes, and sugar and season generously, then stir gently for about 3 minutes until heated through.

3. Meanwhile, cook the pasta in plenty of boiling salted water until tender but still firm to the bite, then drain. Pour the sauce over the pasta, toss gently to avoid breaking the cherry tomatoes and serve with a dollop of crème fraîche (if using).

NOTE
Research suggests that regular consumption of tomatoes, as part of a balanced diet, can lower the risk of prostate cancer. This is due to slycopene—the pigment that gives tomatoes their color.

Green vegetable pesto with gemelli

1. To make the pesto, place the basil, garlic, Parmesan, cashew nuts and oil in a food processor and pulse until smooth. Season to taste and set aside.

2. Meanwhile, bring a saucepan of salted water to the boil. Add the pasta and cook for 6 minutes. Add the beans and cook for 1 minute, then add the rest of the vegetables and cook for a further 2 minutes. Drain thoroughly.

3. Return the pasta and vegetables to the saucepan and stir in the pesto. Heat gently for about 1 minute, until well combined and hot. Serve garnished with extra basil (if using).

NOTE
Traditionally, pesto is made with pine nuts, but you can make it with other nuts too. Why not give brazil nuts, pistachios or cashews a try for a change?

1½ cups gemelli
½ cup halved green beans
½ cup broccoli florets
1 courgette (zucchini), cut into
    matchsticks

PESTO
1 tablespoon fresh basil, plus extra
    leaves to garnish (optional)
1 clove garlic, crushed
4 tablespoons grated Parmesan
    cheese
2 tablespoons cashew nuts
4 tablespoons extra virgin olive oil
sea salt and freshly ground black
    pepper

Fusilli with bell peppers & sun-dried tomatoes

SERVES 4

1 yellow and 1 red bell pepper
   (capsicums)
5 tablespoons extra virgin olive oil
2 French shallots, finely chopped
1 clove garlic, finely chopped
1 teaspoon crushed dried chillies
3½fl oz (100ml) vegetable bouillon
4oz (125g) sun-dried tomatoes in oil,
   drained and chopped
2 tablespoons capers, rinsed and
   dried
2 tablespoons balsamic vinegar
12oz (340g) fusilli
2 tablespoons chopped fresh oregano
   for garnish

1. Preheat the oven to 450°F (230°C). Place the bell peppers in an ovenproof dish and cook for 30 minutes or until soft. Leave to cool for 10 minutes, then remove the skins, deseed and chop.

2. Heat half the oil in a heavy-based saucepan, then add the shallots and cook for 5 minutes or until softened. Add the garlic, chillies and 2 tablespoons of the bouillon and cook for 5 minutes, then add the bell peppers and the sun-dried tomatoes and cook for a further 10 minutes, adding a little more bouillon if the sauce starts to dry out. Mix in the capers and vinegar and cook for 1 minute.

3. Cook the pasta in plenty of boiling salted water until tender but still very firm to the bite. Drain, then toss with the remaining oil. Spoon over the sauce, toss again, then serve at room temperature garnished with the oregano.

NOTE
This brightly colored pasta is great warm, hot or cold. On a summer's day it makes a fabulous pasta salad. If you haven't got any fresh oregano, use basil instead.

Pappardelle with french shallots

1. Put 2oz (60g) of butter, 2 tablespoons of the bouillon and the shallots into a small, heavy-based saucepan. Cover and cook, stirring occasionally, for 5 minutes or until the shallots have softened. Mix in the witlof leaves and cook, uncovered, for 2 minutes. Stir often.

2. Add the peas and half the bouillon to the pan, bring to the boil, then reduce the heat and cook, covered, for 7 minutes or until the peas are tender. Add a little more bouillon if the sauce starts to dry out. Season to taste.

3. Cook the pasta in plenty of boiling salted water until tender but still firm to the bite. Drain, toss with the remaining butter, then spoon over the sauce. Sprinkle with mint and serve with the Parmesan.

3½oz (100g) unsalted butter
70fl oz (200ml) vegetable or chicken bouillon
4 tablespoons finely chopped French shallots
12 witlof leaves, shredded
10oz (285g) shelled fresh peas
salt and freshly ground black pepper
17½oz (500g) fresh pappardelle
2 tablespoons chopped fresh mint for garnish
freshly grated Parmesan cheese to serve

Filini al crudo

SERVES 4

¼ cup olive oil
1 medium onion, chopped finely
8½oz (250g) filini
2 x 14oz (400g) canned chopped
   tomatoes
2oz (60g) black olives, pitted and
   chopped
2oz (60g) capers
¼ teaspoon red chilli flakes
¾ cup dry white wine
½ cup chopped fresh parsley
salt and freshly ground black pepper
   to taste

1. Heat the oil in a heavy-based skillet and sauté the onion until translucent. Add the pasta broken in half, and stir briefly.

2. Add the tomatoes and their juice, together with the olives and capers and stir well.

3. Add the red chilli flakes and stir well to ensure that the pasta is not sticking together.

4. Add the wine and stir again. Cover and simmer for about 20 minutes, stirring to separate pasta if necessary.

5. Add parsley and salt and pepper to taste and cook only until the pasta is tender but still firm to the bite. Do not overcook. The sauce should be quite thick.If you find that there is not enough sauce, add some boiling water, stir to distribute and serve.

NOTE
As the pasta is cooked with the sauce without any pre-cooking at all, you must be careful to ensure that the pasta does not stick together or to the bottom of the pan, and that there is enough liquid in the sauce. You may vary the amount of red chilli flakes, depending on how hot you would like the dish to be.

Stortelli with mixed roasted vegetables

SERVES 4

1. Preheat the oven to 400°F (200°C). Place the tomatoes in a bowl and pour over boiling water. Leave for 30 seconds, then peel, deseed and thickly slice.

2. Place the tomatoes, eggplant, courgette, bell pepper and onions in a shallow roasting tin. Season and drizzle with 2 tablespoons of the oil. Shake the tray gently to cover the vegetables with the oil. Bake for 40 minutes or until the vegetables are tender and slightly browned.

3. Mix together the remaining oil, garlic and basil. Cook the pasta in plenty of boiling salted water until tender but still firm to the bite, then drain. Toss with the basil mixture, spoon onto 4 warmed plates and top with the roasted vegetables. Serve the Parmesan separately.

NOTE
The colors of the roasted vegetables and the flavor of the basil sauce conspire to make this pasta an all-time favorite. You can even eat it cold as a pasta salad.

4 ripe tomatoes
1 small or ½ large eggplant, thickly sliced
1 courgette (zucchini), thickly sliced
1 red or yellow bell pepper (capsicum), cut into quarters
2 red onions, thickly sliced
salt and freshly ground black pepper
5 tablespoons extra virgin olive oil
2 cloves garlic, finely chopped
24 fresh basil leaves, torn
12oz (340g) stortelli
freshly grated Parmesan cheese to serve

Lasagne & green beans with pesto

SERVES 4

2 cups fine green beans, trimmed
salt and freshly ground black pepper
8½oz (250g) fresh lasagne sheets
1 cup pesto
½ cup crème fraîche
4 tablespoons extra virgin olive oil
6 tablespoons walnut pieces
freshly grated Parmesan cheese
    to serve

1. Preheat the oven to 400°F (200°C). Cook the green beans in plenty of boiling salted water for 5 minutes or until tender. Remove the beans from the pot and set aside.

2. Add the lasagne to the boiling water and cook until tender but still firm to the bite. Drain, rinse under cold water and drain again, then pat dry with absorbent paper.

3. Mix together the pesto, crème fraîche, 3 tablespoons of the oil and plenty of pepper. Grease a shallow ovenproof dish with the remaining oil and cover the base with a layer of lasagne sheets. Spread over a little of the pesto mixture, then cover with a layer of green beans and walnuts. Repeat the layers, finishing with the pesto mixture. Bake for 10–15 minutes or until golden. Serve with the Parmesan.

Fusilli with tomato sauce

1. Place the tomatoes in a large, heavy-based saucepan with the tomato paste, sugar, onions, celery, oil, salt and pepper. Cook for 15 minutes or until the onions and celery have softened. Blend to a purée in a food processor or with a hand blender.

2. Return the tomato sauce to the pan, then add the wine. Simmer, uncovered, for 30 minutes or until thickened. Add the butter and stir until melted and combined. Season again to taste.

3. Meanwhile, cook the pasta in plenty of boiling salted water until tender but still firm to the bite, then drain. Pour over the sauce, toss well and serve.

NOTE
This classic tomato sauce for pasta is delicious on its own, but you can use the recipe as a basis for all sorts of other ideas. If you feel like it, add a bit of chilli and basil.

15oz (440g) canned peeled tomatoes
1 teaspoon tomato paste
1 teaspoon sugar
2 onions, chopped
2 sticks celery, chopped
5 tablespoons extra virgin olive oil
salt and freshly ground black pepper
6 tablespoons red wine
4 tablespoons butter
2 cups fusilli

Spaghetti with neapolitan sauce

SERVES 4

21oz (600g) ripe tomatoes
1 clove garlic, finely chopped
1 tablespoon finely chopped onion
2 tablespoons vegetable bouillon
salt and freshly ground black pepper
14oz (400g) dried spaghetti
3½fl oz (100ml) extra virgin olive oil

1. Place the tomatoes in a bowl and cover with boiling water. Leave for 30 seconds, then peel, deseed and roughly chop.

2. Place the garlic, onion, bouillon and 2 pinches of salt in a large saucepan, cover, and cook gently for 5 minutes or until the onion has softened and the liquid has evaporated. Stir in the tomatoes, season with pepper, bring to the boil and cook for 5 minutes or until the tomatoes have softened. Add more salt to taste if necessary.

3. Cook the pasta in plenty of boiling salted water until tender but still firm to the bite, then drain. Toss with the oil, then cover with the sauce and toss again thoroughly. Serve.

Tortellini & avocado cream

1. Cook tortellini in boiling water in a large saucepan following packet directions. Drain, set aside and keep warm.

2. To make avocado cream, place avocado, cream, Parmesan and lemon juice in a food processor or blender and process until smooth. Season to taste with black pepper.

3. Place tortellini in a warm serving bowl, add avocado cream and toss to combine. Serve immediately, garnished with lemon slices and parsley.

17½oz (500g) tortellini

AVOCADO CREAM
½ ripe avocado, pitted and peeled
¼ cup heavy cream
1oz (30g) Parmesan cheese, grated
1 teaspoon lemon juice freshly
   ground black pepper
lemon slice to garnish
fresh parsley leaves for garnish

Rigatoni with squash

SERVES 4

17½oz (500g) rigatoni
3oz (90g) butter
8½oz (250g) squash, cut into small
cubes
1 tablespoon snipped fresh chives
pinch ground nutmeg
1oz (30g) Parmesan cheese, grated
freshly ground black pepper

1. Cook rigatoni in a large saucepan of boiling salted water until tender but still firm to the bite. Drain, set aside and keep warm.
2. Melt 2oz (60g) butter in a large saucepan and cook squash over a medium heat for 5–10 minutes or until tender.
3. Stir chives, nutmeg, Parmesan, black pepper (to taste), rigatoni and remaining butter into squash mixture and toss to combine. Serve immediately.

Tortellini with tomato & cream sauce

SERVES 4

1. Place the butter, onion, celery, tomato sauce and sugar in a heavy-based saucepan and bring to the boil. Reduce the heat and simmer, uncovered, for 30 minutes or until the vegetables have softened and the sauce thickened.

2. Spoon in the crème fraîche, season and bring back to the boil, stirring. Simmer for 1 minute. If necessary, add more salt and pepper.

3. Cook the pasta in plenty of boiling salted water until tender but still firm to the bite, then drain. Transfer to a warmed serving bowl and cover with the sauce. Serve with Parmesan.

NOTE

You can serve all kinds of filled pasta with this creamy tomato sauce, but it goes particularly well with the mixture of spinach and ricotta in these delectable tortellini.

2oz (60g) unsalted butter
1 small onion, finely chopped
1 stick celery, finely chopped
14oz (400g) tomato sauce
½ teaspoons superfine sugar
5fl oz (145ml) crème fraîche
salt and freshly ground black pepper
21oz (600g) fresh spinach and
  ricotta tortellini
freshly grated Parmesan cheese
  to serve

Penne, cauliflower & broccoli bake

SERVES 4

1¼ cups cauliflower florets
1 cup broccoli florets
2 cups penne

CHEESE SAUCE

2 cups low-fat milk
4 tablespoons butter
3 tablespoons all-purpose (plain)
  flour, sieved
8½oz (250g) aged Cheddar cheese,
  grated
1 tablespoon wholegrain mustard
sea salt and freshly ground black
  pepper

TOPPING

4 tablespoons fresh breadcrumbs,
  made from 2 slices stonebaked
  white loaf, crusts removed
2 scallions (spring onions), finely
  chopped
2 tablespoons butter, melted

1. Preheat the oven to 400°F (200°C). Add the cauliflower to a saucepan of boiling water then simmer, covered, for 4 minutes. Add the broccoli to the pan, cover and simmer for a further 2 minutes, then drain well.

2. Meanwhile, make the cheese sauce. Place the milk, butter and flour in a large saucepan and gently heat. Bring slowly to the boil, whisking with a wire whisk, until the mixture thickens. Cook for a further 2 minutes, stirring all the time. Mix in 6oz (170g) of the Cheddar, the mustard and the seasoning, remove from the heat and stir until the Cheddar has melted.

3. Cook the pasta in plenty of boiling salted water until tender but still firm to the bite. Drain and gently mix with the vegetables. Add the cheese sauce to the pasta, mix well, then transfer to an ovenproof dish.

4. Mix all the topping ingredients together with the remaining Cheddar and sprinkle over the pasta. Bake for 15–20 minutes or until the top is golden and bubbling.

NOTE

This satisfying pasta bake, with its cheese sauce and crunchy golden topping, is a great way to get your children to eat vegetables. Grown ups will love it, too.

Roasted squash & sage butter penne

SERVES 4

1. Preheat the oven to 450°F (230°C). Toss together the oil, garlic, half of the chopped fresh sage or dried sage, and the butternut squash. Cook at the top of the oven for 20 minutes or until tender.

2. Meanwhile, cook the pasta in plenty of boiling salted water until tender but still firm to the bite.

3. Melt the butter in a large skillet, add the remaining chopped sage and fry gently for 2–3 minutes. Meanwhile, heat another skillet and dry-fry the pine nuts for 3–4 minutes over a high heat until golden.

4. Drain the pasta, reserving 4 tablespoons of the cooking liquid. Add the reserved liquid to the butter, then add the pasta and cooked squash. Toss, then serve sprinkled with the Parmesan, pine nuts and pepper. Garnish with the sage.

NOTE
Roasted butternut squash has a wonderfully sweet, nutty richness that goes brilliantly with sage and pasta. Serve with a mixed salad and crusty baguette.

2 tablespoons olive oil
2 cloves garlic, chopped
2 tablespoons chopped fresh sage,
*   plus extra sprigs to garnish, or 2*
*   teaspoons dried sage*
1 butternut squash, peeled and cut
*   into ½in (1cm) dice*
2 cups penne
6 tablespoons butter
2 tablespoons pine nuts
salt and freshly ground black pepper
2 tablespoons grated Parmesan
*   cheese*

Penne primavera

4 tablespoons butter

3 cups baby spinach

2 cups fresh shelled peas

2 cups shelled fava beans

4 tablespoons crème fraîche

1 bunch scallions (spring onions),
    finely sliced

2 tablespoons finely chopped fresh
    parsley

salt and freshly ground black pepper

6 tablespoons grated Parmesan
    cheese

3½ cups penne

1. Melt the butter in a saucepan, add the spinach, cover and cook for 5 minutes or until the leaves wilt. Set aside to cool. Cook the peas and beans in a little boiling salted water for 5 minutes or until tender, then drain.

2. Blend the spinach and crème fraîche to a purée in a food processor or with a hand blender. Return the purée to the pan and stir in the peas and beans. Mix in the scallions and parsley, season and add half the Parmesan. Keep warm over a low heat.

3. Meanwhile, cook the pasta in boiling salted water until tender but still firm to the bite. Drain, then toss with the spinach sauce. Serve with the remaining Parmesan.

NOTE

You can use any lightly cooked vegetables or pasta shapes in this springtime dish, but the green shades of peas, spinach, parsley and beans are particularly pretty.

Shell gnocchi with broccoli & golden raisins

SERVES 4

1. Place the raisins in a bowl, cover with hot water and leave to soak for 15 minutes or until they plump up. Drain well. Heat a large heavy-based skillet over a high heat, then add the pine nuts and dry-fry for 2–3 minutes until golden. Remove from the pan and set aside. Cook the broccoli in boiling salted water for 3 minutes, then drain well.

2. Heat the oil in the skillet, then gently fry the onion for 5 minutes or until softened. Add the anchovies and mash well with a fork, then stir in the broccoli, raisins and pine nuts and cook, stirring, for 5 minutes. Season to taste.

3. Cook the pasta in plenty of boiling salted water until tender but still firm to the bite. Drain, return to the pan, then toss with the butter, Parmesan and half the broccoli mixture. Transfer to a bowl and top with the remaining broccoli mixture.

3 tablespoons golden raisins
2 tablespoons pine nuts
17½oz (500g) broccoli, cut into florets
4 tablespoons extra virgin olive oil
1 small onion, thinly sliced
4 anchovy fillets, drained and chopped
salt and freshly ground black pepper
14oz (400g) shell gnocchi
1oz (30g) butter
2oz (60g) Parmesan cheese, grated

meat sauces

Beef ravioli with cream & parmesan

SERVES 4

21¾oz (625g) fresh beef bolognese
    ravioli
7fl oz (200ml) heavy cream
1oz (30g) unsalted butter
freshly ground black pepper
freshly grated nutmeg
2oz (60g) Parmesan cheese, freshly
    grated, plus extra to serve

1. Cook the ravioli in plenty of boiling salted water until tender but still firm to the bite. Meanwhile, place half the cream and the butter in a large heavy-based skillet and heat gently for 1 minute or until the butter has melted.

2. Drain the ravioli and add immediately to the cream and butter mixture. Cook for 30 seconds, stirring, then mix in the remaining cream and plenty of pepper, nutmeg and Parmesan. Toss over the heat for a few seconds until the ravioli are well coated in the sauce, then serve with the extra Parmesan.

NOTE
These ravioli have a wonderfully rich meaty flavor. They are complemented perfectly by a simple sauce of cream with fresh Parmesan and a little warming nutmeg.

Linguine with ham, saffron & cream

SERVES 4

1. Pour 2 tablespoons of boiling water over the saffron and leave to infuse for 10 minutes. Place the cream, ham and Parmesan in a small saucepan and heat gently, but do not allow it to boil. Add the saffron mixture to the cream and ham, season to taste and mix thoroughly.

2. Meanwhile, cook the pasta in plenty of boiling salted water until tender but still firm to the bite. Drain the pasta and transfer half to a serving bowl. Toss with half the sauce, then mix in the remaining pasta. Spoon over the remaining sauce, sprinkle with the parsley and serve with the extra Parmesan.

NOTE
The distinctive flavor of saffron infuses the creamy sauce that coats the pasta in this dish. You can buy thickly sliced ham at the delicatessen counter.

1 teaspoon saffron strands
7fl oz (200ml) heavy cream
5oz (145g) thickly sliced ham, cubed
2oz (60g) Parmesan cheese, freshly
  grated, plus extra to serve
salt and freshly ground black pepper
13oz (370g) dried linguine
2 tablespoons chopped fresh parsley
  to garnish

Tagliatelle with asparagus & prosciutto

SERVES 4

17½oz (500g) asparagus
2oz (60g) unsalted butter
2 tablespoons olive oil
1 scallion, white part only, sliced
2oz (60g) prosciutto, cut into thin
   strips
5fl oz (145ml) heavy cream
salt and freshly ground black pepper
17½oz (500g) fresh tagliatelle
freshly grated Parmesan cheese
   to serve

1. Cut the asparagus spears into ½in (1cm) pieces, leaving the tips whole. Heat the butter and oil in a large, heavy-based skillet, add the scallion and cook for 2 minutes to soften, then mix in the prosciutto. Fry for 2 minutes, then add the asparagus and cook for 5 minutes or until softened, turning occasionally. Pour in the cream and bring to the boil. Season to taste.

2. Meanwhile, cook the pasta in plenty of boiling salted water until tender but still firm to the bite. Drain, reserving some of the cooking water. Transfer one-third of the pasta to a warmed bowl and toss with some of the sauce. Repeat, then spoon the remaining sauce over the top. If the pasta looks a little dry, add 1 or 2 tablespoons of the reserved cooking water. Serve with the Parmesan.

Penne with pancetta & tomatoes

SERVES 4

1.   Heat 2 tablespoons of the oil in a large, heavy-based skillet, then fry the pancetta or bacon and chillies for 2–3 minutes until the fat starts to run out. Add the wine and boil for 2–3 minutes or until reduced by half.

2.   Lower the heat, add the onion and ½ teaspoon of salt to the pancetta and cook, covered, for 8 minutes, stirring occasionally, until the onion has softened. Stir in the tomatoes and cook, covered, for 20–25 minutes or until thickened. If the mixture is a little dry, add 2 tablespoons of hot water. Season if necessary.

3.   Meanwhile, cook the pasta in plenty of boiling salted water until tender but still firm to the bite. Drain, then transfer to a warmed serving bowl. Stir in the remaining oil and half the sauce. Mix, then add 4 tablespoons of Parmesan. Toss, then spoon over the rest of the sauce and serve with the remaining Parmesan.

4 tablespoons extra virgin olive oil
7oz (200g) unsmoked pancetta or rindless lean bacon, roughly chopped
1 teaspoon crushed dried chillies
3½fl oz (100ml) dry white wine
1 sweet or mild onion, very finely chopped
salt
14oz (400g) canned chopped tomatoes
14oz (400g) penne
3oz (90g) Parmesan cheese, freshly grated

Macaroni with lamb ragù

SERVES 4

2 tablespoons olive oil
2oz (60g) butter
1 stick celery, finely chopped
1 onion, finely chopped
1 small carrot, finely chopped
12oz (340g) lean ground lamb
salt and freshly ground black pepper
1 cup full-fat milk
12oz (340g) dried short-cut
   macaroni
2 tablespoons chopped fresh mint to
   garnish
freshly grated Parmesan cheese to
   serve

1. Heat the oil and butter in a large, heavy-based skillet and gently fry the celery, onion and carrot for 5–7 minutes until softened. Add the lamb and cook, stirring, for 5–6 minutes, or until the meat has browned, then season.

2. Reduce the heat to very low and stir in the milk 2–3 tablespoons at a time, ensuring that each addition is absorbed before you add the next. This should take 30 minutes, by which time the vegetables will be tender and the meat cooked.

3. Cook the pasta in plenty of boiling salted water until tender but still firm to the bite, then drain. Mix in 4–5 tablespoons of the sauce, then divide between 4 warmed bowls and spoon over the rest of the sauce. Garnish with mint and serve the Parmesan separately.

NOTE
This pasta's simple meaty sauce is given a lovely richness with the use of a traditional Sardinian technique.

Ham & cheese tortellini with sage butter

1. Place the butter, garlic and sage in a small, heavy-based saucepan and heat over a low heat for 1–2 minutes or until the butter has melted. Season with pepper.

2. Cook the pasta in plenty of boiling salted water until tender but still firm to the bite. Drain and transfer one-third to a warmed bowl. Toss with 1 tablespoon of the sauce and 2 tablespoons of the Parmesan. Repeat with another third of both the pasta and the sauce, then add the remaining pasta and top with the rest of the sauce and the Parmesan. Toss thoroughly, then serve with the extra Parmesan.

NOTE
Fresh sage is the key ingredient in this dish. Without being overpowering, its flavor and aroma turn a classic cheese and ham pasta into something much more unusual.

6 tablespoons butter
1 clove garlic, very finely chopped
20 fresh sage leaves, finely chopped
salt and freshly ground black pepper
8½oz (250g) fresh smoked ham
17½oz (500g) cheese tortellini
4 tablespoons freshly grated Parmesan cheese, plus extra to serve

Tagliatelle with bolognese sauce

SERVES 4

3 tablespoons olive oil

2 tablespoons butter

4oz (125g) unsmoked pancetta or
    rindless bacon, roughly chopped

1 small onion, very finely chopped

1 small carrot, very finely chopped

1 stick celery, very finely chopped

1 small clove garlic, crushed

17½oz (500g) ground beef steak

½ cup dry white wine

2 tablespoons tomato paste

½ cup beef bouillon

salt and freshly ground black pepper

½ cup full-fat milk

17½oz (500g) fresh tagliatelle

freshly grated Parmesan cheese to
    serve

1.   Place the oil, butter, pancetta or bacon, onion, carrot, celery and garlic in a large heavy-based saucepan and cook over a low heat for 5–7 minutes, until the vegetables have softened. Stir from time to time. Add the beef and cook, stirring constantly for 3–5 minutes, or until browned.

2.   Pour in the wine and boil for 2–3 minutes, or until reduced by more than half. Mix in the tomato paste, bouillon and seasoning. Return to the boil, then simmer very gently, uncovered, for 2–2½ hours, stirring from time to time. Add 2 tablespoons of milk whenever the sauce starts to dry out.

3.   Cook the pasta in plenty of boiling salted water until tender but still firm to the bite. Drain, then transfer one-third of the pasta to a warmed serving bowl and spoon over 1 tablespoon of the sauce. Repeat, then add the remaining pasta and toss well. Spoon over the remaining sauce. Serve with the Parmesan.

Spaghetti with ham & mushrooms

SERVES 4

1. Heat the oil and butter in a large, heavy-based skillet. Add the mushrooms, French shallots and ham and fry gently for 2–3 minutes or until lightly colored.

2. Crumble the bouillon cube and add to the mushroom mixture together with the wine. Let the wine bubble for 1–2 minutes, then stir in the tomato sauce and simmer for 2–3 minutes or until the shallots have softened. Season to taste.

3. Meanwhile, cook the pasta in plenty of boiling salted water until tender but still firm to the bite. Drain, reserving a cupful of the cooking water. Add pasta to the mushroom and tomato mixture and toss for 1 minute. If the dish seems a little dry, add a few tablespoons of the reserved pasta water. Serve with the Parmesan.

NOTE
This dish is called spaghetti alla boscaiola in Italy. A boscaiolo is a woodsman who loves mushrooms. In this recipe, the mushroom are combined with ham in a rich tomato sauce.

4 tablespoons extra virgin olive oil
2oz (60g) unsalted butter
3½oz (100g) Swiss brown cup mushrooms, sliced
2 French shallots, very finely chopped
5oz (145g) thick-cut cooked ham, chopped
1 beef bouillon cube
6 tablespoons red wine
5 tablespoons tomato sauce
salt and freshly ground black pepper
17½oz (500g) fresh spaghetti
freshly grated Parmesan cheese to serve

Penne with bacon & chicken livers

SERVES 4

2 tablespoons vegetable oil
4 rashers rindless bacon, chopped
1 small onion, finely chopped
1 clove garlic, crushed
8½oz (250g) frozen chicken livers,
    defrosted and chopped
2 teaspoons all-purpose (plain) flour
¾ cup chicken bouillon
1 tablespoon tomato paste
½ teaspoons dried marjoram
salt and freshly ground black pepper
17½oz (500g) penne
3 tablespoons sour cream
chopped fresh basil or parsley for
    garnish

1. Heat the oil in a large heavy-based skillet and cook the bacon, onion and garlic for 4–5 minutes until softened. Add the chicken livers and cook, stirring, for 3 minutes or until they start to brown.

2. Stir in the flour. Gradually add the bouillon, stirring all the time. Stir in the tomato paste, marjoram and seasoning. Cover the skillet and simmer for 10 minutes or until the chicken livers are tender and cooked through.

3. Meanwhile, cook the pasta in plenty of boiling salted water until tender but still firm to the bite. Drain well and transfer to a serving dish. Stir the sour cream into the sauce, then pour the sauce over the pasta and garnish with the basil or parsley.

NOTE
Chicken livers, bacon, and a little sour cream make a wonderfully rich and tasty pasta sauce. But take care not to overcook the livers or they'll become tough and dry.

Tagliatelle & meatballs with spicy tomato sauce

1. Place the breadcrumbs in a large bowl and combine with the ground beef, bacon, onion, parsley, egg and seasoning and mix well. Shape the mixture into 20 balls, and then flatten slightly with the palm of your hand. Chill in the refrigerator for 10 minutes.

2. Heat the oil in a large skillet and over a medium–high heat brown the meatballs on all sides for about 5 minutes (you may need to do this in 2 batches). Spoon off any excess oil from the skillet and pour the pasta sauce over the meatballs in the pan. Reduce the heat to medium and simmer gently for 10 minutes, turning the meatballs occasionally, until cooked through.

3. Meanwhile, cook the pasta in plenty of boiling salted water until tender but still firm to the bite, then drain. Serve the meatballs with the pasta and garnish with the extra parsley.

1 cup fresh breadcrumbs, made from 2 slices stonebaked white loaf, crusts removed

17½oz (500g) ground beef

½ cup finely chopped bacon

1 small onion, finely chopped

3 tablespoons chopped fresh parsley, plus extra for garnish

1 medium egg, beaten

sea salt and freshly ground black pepper

2 tablespoons sunflower oil

2 cups bottled spicy roasted garlic pasta sauce

17½oz (500g) tagliatelle

poultry sauces

Chicken & mushroom linguine

SERVES 4

1 tablespoon sunflower oil
2 skinless chicken breasts
6 cloves garlic, unpeeled
8½oz (250g) Swiss brown cup
    mushrooms or wild mushrooms,
    such as chanterelles, sliced
7fl oz (200ml) heavy cream
salt and freshly ground black pepper
17½oz (500g) fresh linguine
1½oz (45g) unsalted butter
4 tablespoons freshly grated
    Parmesan cheese

1. Preheat the oven to 400°F (200°C). Heat the oil in a large, heavy-based skillet, add the chicken and fry for 1 minute on each side or until browned. Cut each breast in half, then lay in a single layer in an ovenproof dish.

2. Add the garlic to the skillet and fry over gentle heat for 3 minutes or until softened. Remove from the skillet, leave to cool slightly, then peel, crush and add to the chicken together with the mushrooms, cream and seasoning. Cover the dish with foil and bake for 20 minutes or until the chicken is tender and cooked through.

3. Cook the pasta in plenty of boiling salted water until tender but still firm to the bite. Drain, then return to the skillet and toss with the butter and Parmesan. Transfer to a serving dish, then spoon the chicken and mushroom mixture over the top.

Chicken cannelloni

1. Preheat the oven to 350°F (180°C). Heat oil or butter in a large skillet, add onion and sauté for 2 minutes. Then add chicken, veal and bacon and stir until browned. Add tomato paste, water, salt and pepper to taste and nutmeg.

2. To make the béchamel sauce, melt the 6oz (170g) butter in a skillet, add flour and stir for 1 minute. Remove from heat and gradually add milk, stirring well. Return to heat and stir until sauce thickens and boils. Remove from heat, stir in nutmeg, seasonings, cheese and eggs. Remove ½ cup of sauce and stir it into the mince mixture.

3. Fill cannelloni tubes with meat mixture. Grease a large ovenproof dish. Mix pasta sauce and water together and spread half over base of dish. Place filled cannelloni tubes in two rows in the dish then pour over remaining pasta sauce. Pour over the béchamel sauce, spread evenly and sprinkle with a little grated Parmesan.

4. Dot with butter and bake for 30–35 minutes or until golden brown. Serve hot with a tossed salad.

2 tablespoons olive oil or butter
1 onion, finely chopped
8½oz (250g) ground chicken
8½oz (250g) ground veal
2 tablespoons tomato paste
½ cup water
salt and freshly ground black pepper
¼ teaspoon nutmeg
packet cannelloni tubes
1½ cups bottled pasta sauce
½ cup water
freshly grated Parmesan cheese to
   top
2 teaspoons butter to top

BÉCHAMEL SAUCE
6oz (170g) butter
¾ cup all-purpose (plain) flour
4 cups milk
⅛ teaspoon nutmeg
salt and freshly ground black pepper
3 tablespoons grated Parmesan
   cheese
2 eggs, beaten

Penne with curried chicken

SERVES 4

3 tablespoons golden raisins
2oz (60g) unsalted butter
1 tablespoon olive oil
½ cup crème fraîche
½ cup dry white wine
2 tablespoons milk
1 tablespoon curry powder or to
   taste
1 large clove garlic, very finely
   chopped
2 bay leaves
salt
2oz (60g) ground almonds
10½oz (300g) roast chicken breast
   fillets, skinned and cut into small
   strips
17½oz (500g) penne

1. Place the raisins in a bowl, cover with boiling water and leave for 15 minutes or until plump. Drain.

2. Place the butter, oil, crème fraîche, wine, milk, curry powder, garlic, bay leaves and salt in a heavy-based skillet. Bring to the boil, then simmer, uncovered, for 15–20 minutes, stirring from time to time or until the sauce has reduced considerably.

3. Stir in the almonds, raisins and chicken strips. Adjust the seasoning and cook for 2–3 minutes or until heated through.

4. While the sauce is simmering, cook the pasta in plenty of boiling salted water until tender but still firm to the bite, then drain. Transfer to a warmed bowl. Discard the bay leaves and spoon half the sauce over the pasta. Toss well, then spoon over the remaining sauce.

Fettuccine with chicken & avocado sauce

SERVES 4

1. Cook the fettuccine in plenty of boiling salted water until tender but still firm to the bite.

2. Heat oil in a skillet. Add scallions, pine nuts or slivered almonds and chicken and cook until chicken is browned. Stir constantly.

3. Combine white wine and cornstarch, then add cream and egg yolk and pour into skillet. Stir over a medium heat until thickened. Do not boil.

4. Stir in avocado and heat through for 1–2 minutes. Toss a little butter or olive oil through the hot pasta.

5. Serve sauce spooned over cooked pasta and sprinkled with chopped parsley.

17½oz (500g) fettuccine

2 teaspoons olive oil

6 scallions (spring onions), chopped

¼ cup pine nuts or slivered almonds

8½oz (250g) chicken fillets, cut into thin strips

2 tablespoons dry white wine

3 teaspoons cornstarch

¾ cup cream

1 egg yolk, lightly beaten

1 small avocado, diced

2 tablespoons finely chopped fresh parsley

Spanish chicken & mussel spaghetti

SERVES 4

12oz (340g) dried spaghetti
21oz (600g) fresh mussels
2 tablespoons olive oil, plus
   1 tablespoon extra for drizzling
2 scallions (spring onions), finely
   chopped
4 cloves garlic, chopped
¾ cup dry white wine
21oz (600g) chicken thigh pieces,
   cut into small cubes
grated zest of ½ lemon
½ teaspoon dried chilli flakes
2 tablespoons chopped fresh parsley
salt and freshly ground black pepper

1. Cook the spaghetti in plenty of boiling salted water until tender but still firm to the bite, then drain well. Meanwhile, scrub the mussels under cold running water and pull away the beards.Discard any mussels that are open or damaged.

2. Place the mussels in a large, heavy-based skillet, with just the water that is clinging to the shells. Steam for 3–4 minutes over a high heat, shaking regularly, until the shells have opened. Discard any mussels that remain closed.

3. Heat 2 tablespoons of olive oil in a large skillet and gently fry the scallions and garlic for 5 minutes or until softened. Add the wine and chicken pieces and boil rapidly for 5–6 minutes or until the liquid has reduced by half. Add the mussels, lemon zest and chilli, and heat for 2–3 minutes. Add the pasta to the mussels, then stir in the parsley, salt and pepper. Gently toss over the heat and drizzle over the remaining oil.

NOTE
A little bit of chilli adds a spicy bite to the mussels, while garlic, parsley and scallions mingle with the spaghetti. This dish is perfect served with fresh crusty bread.

Smoked chicken pappardelle

SERVES 6

1. To make nasturtium butter, place butter, garlic, lime juice and flowers in a bowl, mix well to combine and set aside.

2. Cook the pasta in plenty of boiling salted water until tender but still firm to the bite. Drain, set aside and keep warm.

3. Heat a non-stick skillet over a medium heat, add chicken and cook, stirring, for 1 minute. Add wine, cream, chives and black pepper to taste, bring to a simmer and cook for 2 minutes. To serve, top pasta with chicken mixture and nasturtium butter.

24oz (750g) pappardelle
3lb 5oz (1.5kg) smoked chicken, skin
    removed and flesh sliced
½ cup dry white wine
1 cup cream
2 tablespoons snipped fresh chives
freshly ground black pepper

NASTURTIUM BUTTER

4oz (125g) butter, softened
1 clove garlic, crushed
1 tablespoon lime juice
6 nasturtium flowers, finely chopped

seafood sauces

Spicy shrimp & scallop spaghetti

SERVES 4

17½oz (500g) green shrimps
8½oz (250g) scallops without corals
12oz (340g) spaghetti
1oz (30g) olive oil spread
2 teaspoons olive oil
2 cloves garlic, crushed
3 scallions (spring onions), sliced
1 small red chilli, finely chopped
½ cup dry white wine
2 large, vine-ripened tomatoes,
    seeded and finely chopped
1 teaspoon lemon zest
1 teaspoon orange zest
1 teaspoon sugar
1 tablespoon chopped fresh chives

1. Peel and devein the shrimps, leaving the tails intact. Pat the scallops dry with paper towel.

2. Cook the spaghetti in a large pot of rapidly boiling salted water until tender but still firm to the bite. Drain, cover and keep warm.

3. Heat the olive oil spread and olive oil in a large, deep skillet and cook the shrimps and scallops in batches over a high heat until just tender. Remove and keep warm.

4. Add the garlic, scallions and chilli to the skillet and cook over a medium heat until the scallions are soft. Stir in the wine and bring to the boil, stirring to release any juices that may be stuck to the bottom of the skillet. Boil until reduced by half.

5. Add the tomatoes, zest, sugar and chives to the skillet and cook just until the tomato is warmed through.

6. Add the shrimps, scallops and spaghetti and toss to combine. Serve with crusty bread.

Tuna spaghetti

SERVES 4

1. Heat the oil in a large, heavy-based skillet, then gently fry the onion for 5–7 minutes or until softened. Add the garlic and anchovies and fry for 2 minutes or until the anchovies have disintegrated.

2. Increase the heat and stir in the tomatoes. Simmer, uncovered, for 5 minutes. Add the tuna and plenty of pepper. Mix together well, then reduce the heat and simmer for 20–25 minutes or until the sauce has thickened.

3. Meanwhile, cook the pasta in plenty of boiling salted water until tender but still firm to the bite, then drain. Transfer to a warmed serving bowl, cover with the sauce and toss well. Sprinkle the parsley over before serving.

3½fl oz (100ml) extra virgin olive oil
1 small onion, chopped
2 cloves garlic, chopped
6 anchovy fillets, drained
14oz (400g) canned chopped tomatoes
6oz (170g) canned tuna chunks in olive oil, drained and flaked
freshly ground black pepper
12oz (340g) spaghetti
3 tablespoons chopped Italian parsley

Fresh crab tagliatelle

SERVES 4

12oz (340g) tagliatelle
3 tablespoons olive oil
2 cloves garlic, chopped
1 red chilli, chopped
finely grated zest of 1 lemon
2 fresh dressed crabs, to give about
    10½oz (300g) crabmeat
7fl oz (200ml) heavy cream
1 tablespoon lemon juice
salt and freshly ground black pepper
2 tablespoons chopped fresh parsley
    to garnish

1. Cook the pasta in plenty of boiling salted water until tender but still firm to the bite, then drain.

2. Meanwhile, heat the oil in a large, heavy-based skillet and gently fry the garlic, chilli and lemon zest for 3–4 minutes until softened but not browned. Add the crabmeat, cream and lemon juice, and simmer for 1–2 minutes to heat through. Season to taste.

3. Transfer the pasta to serving bowls. Spoon the crab mixture over the top and sprinkle with the parsley to garnish.

NOTE
This recipe really makes the most of the fantastic flavor of fresh crab. By using ready-dressed crabs, you take all the hard work out of making this exotic pasta dish.

Smoked salmon fettuccine with peas

SERVES 6

1. Cook the fettuccine in plenty of boiling salted water until tender but still firm to the bite. Drain, set aside and keep warm.

2. To make the sauce, blanch the peas in boiling water for 2 minutes. Refresh under cold running water, drain and set aside. Place the wine in a large skillet and bring to the boil. Stir in 1 cup cream and boil until the sauce reduces and thickens. Place 4 slices of the smoked salmon, scallions and remaining cream in a food processor and purée. Stir the smoked salmon mixture into the sauce and cook until the sauce is hot.

3. Cut the remaining salmon slices into strips. Add the salmon strips and peas to the sauce and season to taste with black pepper. Spoon the sauce over the fettuccine and toss to combine. Serve immediately.

17½oz (500g) fettuccine

SMOKED SALMON SAUCE
4oz (125g) fresh or frozen peas
¼ cup dry white wine
1¼ cups heavy cream
8 slices smoked salmon
3 scallions (spring onions), finely chopped
freshly ground black pepper

Spaghetti with mussels

SERVES 4

4lb 6oz (2kg) mussels
½ cup extra virgin olive oil
12oz (340g) spaghetti
3½fl oz (100ml) dry white wine
2oz (60g) chopped fresh parsley
2 cloves garlic, chopped
1 teaspoon crushed dried chillies

1. Scrub the mussels under cold running water, pull away any beards and discard any mussels that are open or damaged. Place 2 tablespoons of the oil in a large, heavy-based skillet, then add the mussels. Cook, covered, shaking the skillet frequently for 2–4 minutes or until the mussels open. Discard any mussels that do not open.

2. Reserve 12 mussels in their shells for garnishing. Detach the remaining mussels from their shells and set aside. Discard the shells.

3. Cook the pasta in plenty of boiling salted water until tender but still firm to the bite, then drain. Meanwhile, place the remaining oil, the wine, parsley, garlic and chilli in a large, heavy-based skillet and bring to the boil. Cook for 2 minutes to boil off the alcohol. Stir the mussels and pasta into the oil and chilli mixture and toss for 30 seconds to heat through. Serve garnished with the reserved mussels.

NOTE
This classic dish from Naples is a wonderful mix of fresh mussels, wine, garlic and parsley. You can use clams instead of mussels if you like; they are equally good.

Index

Published in 2013 by
New Holland Publishers
London • Sydney • Cape Town • Auckland

Garfield House 86–88 Edgware Road London W2 2EA United Kingdom
1/66 Gibbes Street Chatswood NSW 2067 Australia
Wembley Square First Floor Solan Road Gardens Cape Town 8001 South Africa
218 Lake Road Northcote Auckland New Zealand

Copyright © 2013 New Holland Publishers

www.newhollandpublishers.com

All rights reserved. No part of this publication may be reproduced, stored in a retrieval system
or transmitted, in any form or by any means, electronic, mechanical, photocopying, recording or
otherwise, without the prior written permission of the publishers and copyright holders.

A catalogue record of this book is available at the British Library and the National Library
of Australia.

ISBN: 9781742573861

Publisher: Fiona Schultz
Design: Lorena Susak
Production Director: Olga Dementiev
Printer: Toppan Leefung Printing Ltd (China)

10 9 8 7 6 5 4 3 2 1

Follow New Holland Publishers on
Facebook: www.facebook.com/NewHollandPublishers

MP iA

V

VAPIH

UK £9.99
US $14.99